PRAISE FOR
MINDFUL WRITING FROM THE COUNTY JAIL

"Mindful Writing from the County Jail is a must read if you want to gain insight into the people who are the victims of America's mass incarceration crisis. The writing from these jail detainees is powerful, painful, and poignant. They are our neighbors, and they will be again. They are artists and workers, fathers and brothers. Their humanity spills forward in the words they wrote."

—Pulitzer Prize Winning Columnist Tony Messenger, Author of Profit and Punishment: How America Criminalizes the Poor in the Name of Justice.

"Since FreeWriters has been involved with our patients in jail, there have been considerably less acute mental health request related to anxiety from isolation. I have also witnessed more camaraderie within the housing units of participants."

—Ben Lommen, BSN, RN, PHN Senior Mental Health Nurse, Hennepin Health Equity Jail Services.

"All the incarcerated have a story, and all need to engage through storytelling and other arts to become free. Write it down. Perform it. Paint the picture. Let the tears flow and heal. So, when the cage door finally opens, a butterfly emerges, not the same unformed creature that entered. *Mindful Writing from the County Jail* is a remarkable compilation of that telling, FreeWriters program the necessary means."

—James P. Lenfestey, Minnesota Book Kay Sexton Award Winner, Author of Into the Goodhue County Jail: Poems to Free Prisoners

"Our community programs share the same artistic message of HOPE, LOVE, FORGIVENESS, BELIEF AND JOY. FreeWriters, through mindful writing in the jails and Artfully United, through murals painted on walls, involving at risk community members. I'm happy to have an arts partnership that positively impacts the wellbeing of those they serve."

—Michael Norvice, Renowned Muralist, Founder of ArtfullyUnited.org

"I have learned that both joy and pain are an integral part of our unpredictable journey through life. That no matter how far we've fallen, there is an opportunity to soar if given a helping hand. FreeWriters is that hand, a hand with a pencil that stirs the realm of possibility and helps chart a life of purpose."

—David McNally, Best Selling Author of Even Eagles Need a Push Series.

"The stories presented in this marvelously curated publication echo the voices I have heard from the bench countless times over the years. Perhaps these heart wrenching accounts will allow you to ascertain, as I have, that those in our jails are unique individuals and not criminals in the aggregate. Further we must never imprison a mind. If reform is to take hold, we are obliged to offer programs that reflect dignity, opportunity and incite hope. A mission FreeWriters has dutifully undertaken."

—Burt Riskedahl, Retired District Judge, North Dakota

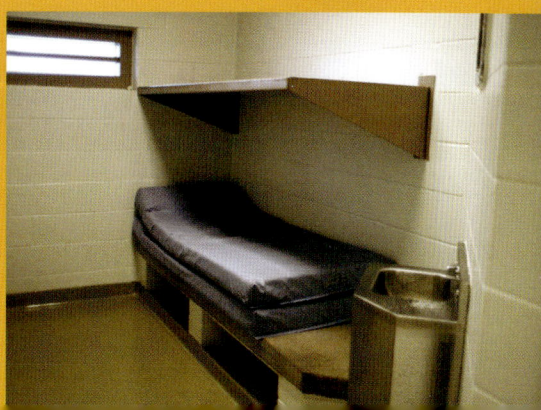

ALL INMATES WILL BE SEARCHED
ENTERIN AND LEAVING
HOUSIN AREA

HENNEPIN
COUNTY JAIL - L
HENNEPIN
COUNTY JAIL - XL

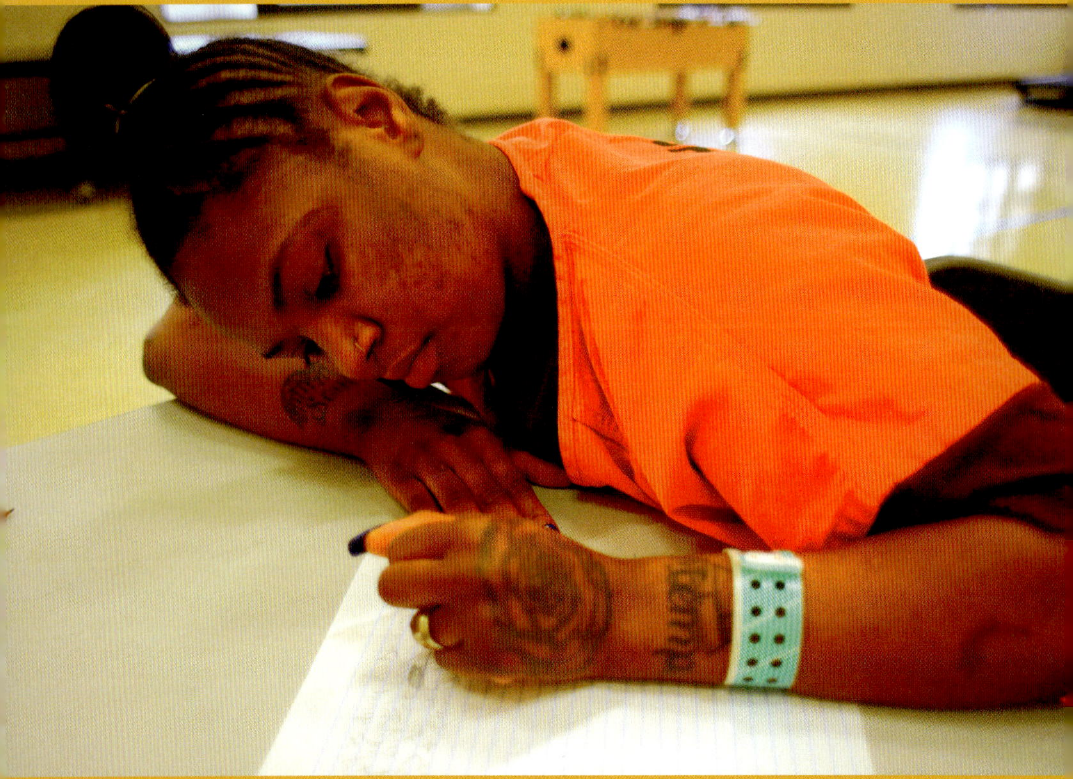

HC SO J-63
JAIL

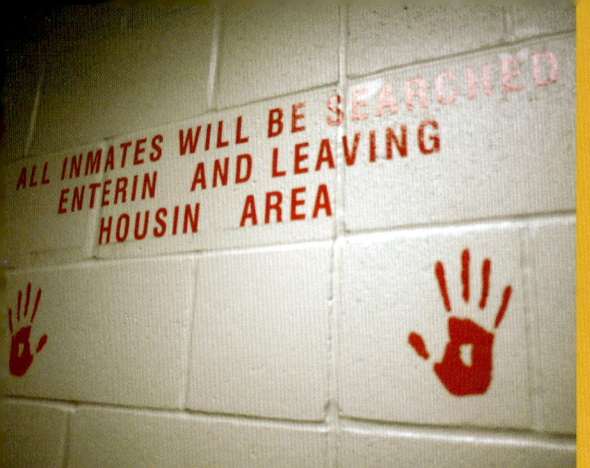

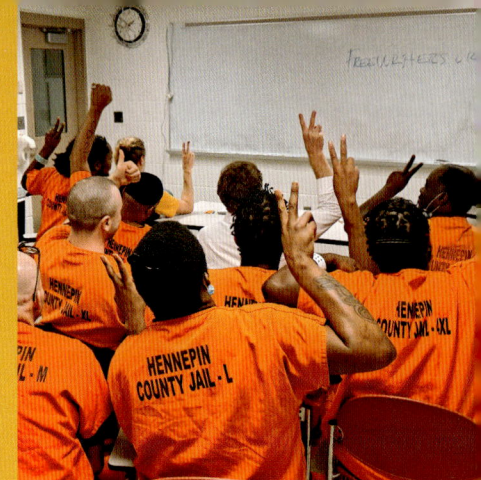

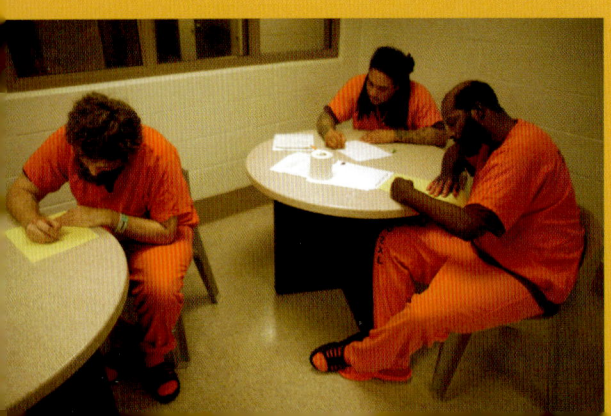

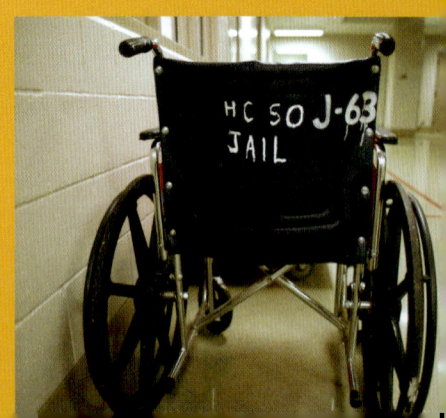

MINDFUL WRITING

from the County Jail

Thank you for supporting "A Write to Hope!"

— Dennis Kelly

A FREEWRITERS COLLECTION

Mindful Writing from the County Jail: A FreeWriters Collection. Copyright © 2024, Dennis Kelly and Dymaxion Press. All rights reserved. No part of this book may be reproduced in any form or by any electronic or mechanical means, including information storage and retrieval systems, without permission in writing except by a reviewer who may quote brief passages in a review.

First Edition published in the United States of America

Submissions: The submissions herein have been donated without compensation for the purpose of publication in print or digital form. Further, the identities of the Mindful Writing authors, who are pre-sentence jail detainees, have been withheld from publication to protect the submitters' privacy.

Editing: Our editors are careful not to alter a writer's opinions or "voice," but all submissions are edited for clarity and precision of language and for logic of argumentation and organization. They are also copy edited for grammar and style and may be adjusted to fit the space available in the publication.

This publication is funded through donations to FreeWriters, a 501(c)3 nonprofit organization.

Executive Editor and Curator: Dennis Kelly

Editorial Support: Nina Resor, Chris Elias, Tina Applebee, Daniel Kendle, Mary Wynne, Norma Bourland, and Melissa Martinez

Book Design and Production: Mayfly Design

Photography: David Guttenfelder and Damian Johansson. See Acknowledgments.

Cover Illustration: Hannah K. Lee (hannahklee.com). Her work has circulated through Printed Matter and has been collected by the libraries of the Museum of Modern Art and the San Francisco Museum of Modern Art, and by the Library of Congress.

Interior Illustrations: All interior illustrations are the work of artists who are or have been incarcerated. See Acknowledgements.

ISBNs: 979-8-218-33540-3 (hc); 979-8-218-26108-5 (pbk)

Dymaxion Press

Our Mission

*To provide incarcerated men and women
with mindful writing opportunities
that improve mental health,
inspire hope, and reduce recidivism.*

Contents

Foreword: James W. Pennebaker, Professor Emeritus of Psychology xv
Founder's Message: Nate Johnson, Founder xvii
Introduction: Dennis Kelly, Senior Instructor xxi
Reflection: Stephan Oseghale, FreeWriters Participant xxvi
How to Read This Collection: Editor's Note xxviii

Prompt 1: I'm From

The Hood 2
Streets 2
Kings 3
Anonymous 3
Lost 4
3 A.M. 4
Beauty 5
Old School 5
Culture 6
Unknown 6
No Doors 7
Bottom Rung 7

Prompt 2: I Am

Big Rig 10
Divine 10
Don't Matter 11
Still the Man 11
Good Kid 12
If You Let Me 12
Who 13
Career 13
Music 14
Friend 14
Lamb 15
Hands 15

Prompt 3: I Remember

Rez Dogs 18
Other Me 18
I Forgot 19
Children 19
When I Was a Girl 20
First Sip 20
Dad 21
Hard Lessons 21
Legacy 21

Prompt 4: Jail

Fork 24
Touch 24
What I Want 25
Concoctions 25
Saved 26
Cage 26
In the Moment 26
Dreams 27
Stress 27
Closed Heart 28
Beautiful Day 28
Pod 7A 29
23 & 1 29

Prompt 5: Letters

Cursive 32
Ask Me 32
Self 33
Pickled 33
In Touch 34
Face-to-Face 34
Open Letter 35
Better Late 35
To My Twelve-Year-Old Self 36

    For You 36
    Passages 37
    Stunned 37

Prompt 6: Broken

    Recommend 40
    Shattered 40
    Plank 41
    Trust 41
    Freedom 42
    Restless 42
    My Story 43
    Fentanyl 43
    Delay-Delay-Delay 44
    Older 44
    Escape 45
    Bounty Hunter 45

Prompt 7: Forgiveness

    The Judge 48
    Making Sense 48
    Why We're Here 49
    When I Said "No" 49
    Courage 50
    Could It Be? 50
    Thanksgiving 51
    Luck 51
    Meds 52
    Anger 52
    Different 53

Prompt 8: Choice

Resolution 56
Freedom 56
Same Old 57
What If? 57
This Life 58
No Tears 58
Goals 59
Don't Ask Me 59
Release 60
Stop 60
Chase 61
Ride 61

Prompt 9: Family

Visitors 64
Burden 65
Success 65
Holding It In 66
Pieces 66
The Day I Was Born 67
Feet Forward 67
Why 68
Grandma 68
Help 69
Hardest Thing 69

Prompt 10: When I Get Out

I'm Going 72
Nope 72
Perfect Day 73
What I Want 73
Hugs 74
Running 74
How Do I Know? 75
Messy 75
Self-Care 76

Change 76
Not Wrong 77
Ten Years 77

Prompt 11: Dear Congressman Phillips

Vision 80
Mental Health 80
Emotions 81
White House 81
Power 82
Brown Men 82
Politician 82
Why? 83
Change 83

Prompt 12: Mindful Writing

Participant Reflections 86

The On-Ramp To Success 91
Acknowledgements 95
Donors 98
Your Support Matters 99

Foreword

James W. Pennebaker,
Professor Emeritus of Psychology

Words that Heal

I hope my scientific colleagues and students read the stunning essays in *Mindful Writing from the County Jail: A FreeWriters Collection*. This powerful book reveals people at their most vulnerable and honest moments. The stories are sometimes horrifying, sad, and scary but, at the same time, honorable, hopeful, and healing. What the collection reveals at the human level is what I've been trying to capture in the scientific world. How can writing about heartbreaking upheavals ultimately be healing?

Almost forty years ago, my students and I began a series of studies where we asked people to write for fifteen to twenty minutes for only three to four days about a deeply upsetting experience that they hadn't talked about with others. By measuring people's visits to doctors and even their immune system activity, we discovered that writing about major upheavals resulted in improvements in both physical and mental health.

In the years since, over a thousand experiments have been conducted on expressive writing. For young and old, rich and poor, in prisons and in board rooms, in countries around the world, putting emotional experiences into words can change lives. Why does it work? Read the essays in this collection and you will see the process in action.

Years of research have found several reasons why writing works. When we put our deepest thoughts and feelings into words, we are publicly acknowledging what has happened to us. We are forced to see who we have been and who we are. We often see ourselves and our situation from another perspective. Above all, writing often helps us to find meaning to our experiences.

There's another important ingredient. After we have written about deeply meaningful events, we are able to see our lives and the worlds around us more clearly. We are more open to talking with others about some of the secrets we've kept to ourselves. We are more connected with others. Writing can make us better friends and more forgiving of others (and ourselves).

Reading the FreeWriters Collection was a powerful experience for me. I've known the science for decades. But reading the stories was a moving reminder of the value of writing. At the same time, it exposes our flawed criminal justice and mental health systems. I encourage you to support programs such as FreeWriters in your community.

James W. Pennebaker is a Professor Emeritus of Psychology at University of Texas at Austin. His publications include: *Opening up by writing it down: How expressive writing improves health and eases emotional pain.* (2016). Pennebaker, J. W., & Smyth, J. M. (2016). New York: Guilford Publications. *Expressive Writing: Words that Heal:* Pennebaker, J.W. and John Evans. (2014). Idyll Arbor Publication

Founder's Message

Nate Johnson

This FreeWriters collection, hopefully the first of many, is dedicated to my friend and spiritual brother, Mr. Joseph Bunce. Joe helped lead me to this work, and his life and spirit continue to inspire my efforts and propel the FreeWriters movement forward. Here's a little bit about how the movement got its start and where it's headed.

A few years before COVID-19 or George Floyd's murder, I lived in southern Minnesota and served unhappily as an assistant county attorney with the vague and perhaps naïve goal of sending lawbreakers to treatment rather than jail or prison. I was several years sober at the time but had not yet seriously faced down my depression and anxiety issues.

Joe Bunce and I met at an AA meeting just as I was considering quitting my prosecutor job and moving back to Minneapolis. Joe was on probation for some DWI and marijuana charges in Blue Earth County.

He was court-ordered to attend his first few AA meetings, but at some point, he decided he liked sobriety and began to look in earnest for a sponsor. I was lucky enough to be there when he reached out for help. I was in a dark place spiritually and emotionally, and I was looking for a healthy way to take periodic breaks from my ruminations.

I quit my job and moved back to Minneapolis in early 2019. Joe and I continued to meet and talk regularly. Unemployed and unsure whether to keep practicing law, I took a writing workshop at the Loft Literary Center. While at the Loft, I learned about "free-writing," which is a mindful, five-minute, spontaneous writing exercise with an optional performance component.

The workshop taught us free-writing as a means of making a first draft of a poem, but I also found it to be a great tool for stress relief (i.e., escaping ruminations). So, I took up the practice in my spare time and formed a writing group to share it with others.

Around that time, Joe relapsed, violated probation, and received a 60-day jail sanction. The first time I visited Joe in jail, I learned disturbing things about the county jail environment—things I didn't know (but certainly should have known) even as a prosecutor. For instance, the detainees had no outdoor time or fresh air, no windows, and no therapeutic or rehabilitative programming other than occasional Bible study and 12-step meetings.

Concerned for Joe's mental health, I showed him the free-writing method, and he took to it immediately. He free-wrote during difficult moments in jail, and the writing helped. I visited Joe as often as I could, each time presenting myself as an attorney, which gave us access to a quiet, confidential space to hug, laugh, cry, and read our free-writes aloud to each other.

Near the end of Joe's sentence, I asked if he thought the other guys in his jail quad would like free-writing. He said he was sure they would, and the FreeWriters concept was born.

I had a friend working at the Hennepin County Sheriff's Office at the time, so I pitched him my idea to lead free-writing classes in the downtown Minneapolis jail. He authorized a few pilot classes, which would entail three five-minute writing and performing exercises in an hour for up to a dozen participants. The classes were a huge hit, and they remain to this day. We now lead eight to twelve FreeWriters jail classes per week in the Twin Cities Metro.

FreeWriters has served over 5,000 incarcerated writers over the past three years, who have composed and performed more than 15,000 pieces of writing, and we now offer twice-monthly, post-incarceration FreeWriters classes for our fellow writers coming out of lockup. This method lifts spirits and eases pain for people who sorely need it—people presumed innocent who lack the funds to post bail and sit for months on end in windowless rooms awaiting trial, and people (95 percent of whom will soon be back in the community) who regularly tell us they would go crazy without these writing groups.

FreeWriters is a pioneering movement, for two reasons. First, at the time of this publication, we are the only mindfulness-based creative arts program able to work consistently and effectively in Twin Cities county jail facilities. Because the average jail term is significantly shorter than the average prison term (jails are for people awaiting their day in court who can't afford bail; prisons are for people serving felony conviction terms), teaching artists who want to lead curriculum-based classes in correctional facilities gravitate toward prisons. The FreeWriters method succeeds in pre-trial county jail settings because participants can derive tremendous therapeutic benefits from one class—indeed, from one free-write. Furthermore, unlike other creative mediums, our only "overhead" is paper, pencils, and a hard surface on which to write.

Second, because FreeWriters classes provide a means and a safe space to be vulnerable—to be "real"—we establish trust relationships each week with dozens of good people soon to be released from jail, more and more of whom connect with us when they're back in the community. We hope to hire and train some of these individuals to lead their own FreeWriters groups—perhaps eventually for the youth in their networks!

FreeWriters understands that most people end up in jail primarily because of what *happened* to them rather than because of what is *wrong* with them. Our mindful writing practice offers each participant an opportunity to unpack long-held feelings of fear, guilt, shame, inadequacy, and past trauma without resistance or judgment. As lifelong layers of tension unravel (in the words of one writer, "I felt like a 50-pound weight just got lifted"), we see people rediscover sources of confidence and self-respect in real time.

Many of our participants, some of whom have young children, find themselves on a fast track to picking up work-related (i.e., organized crime-related) felony convictions, and a felony on their record means severely limited work and housing options, basically forever. However, some have not yet reached this tragic, life-altering (and hugely-expensive-for-taxpayers) stage. FreeWriters exists to connect with these young men and women and offer them something like an off-ramp—a chance to pause, breathe, write, be real, be human, and share their truth; an opportunity to find support, encouragement, a measure of healing, and perhaps a vision for a less perilous path in life.

We intend for our FreeWriters movement to exist as long as poverty breeds incarceration and incarceration breeds poverty. With your help, we believe we will soon be able to grow and serve urban jail populations across the country.

Introduction

Dennis Kelly, FreeWriters Senior Instructor

When I started as a FreeWriters volunteer instructor, I remember thinking, "This is such a good fit!" I was enthusiastic. I understood the FreeWriters mission. I felt well-prepared to facilitate mindful writing practice. After all, I'm a published author, I've taught meditation, and I studied with the godmother of mindful writing, Natalie Goldberg.

I was excited to see how the jail detainees would take to mindful writing.[1] A healing practice that provides the freedom to express one's deepest thoughts and feelings. A cathartic opportunity to put some distance between you and your story, opening space for objective reflection. A path forward, that leaves a perilous past behind and charts a fresh course forward.

However, shortly after I began facilitating writing sessions in the jail, something felt off—an inadequacy on which I couldn't quite put my finger. Maybe it was the disquieting environment: the probing metal detectors, stark concrete walls, clanging of gray steel doors, pervasive cameras, and the headache that always ensued from the absence of windows and the flickering brightness of overhead lights.

Or, perhaps it was the alarming in-custody stats. Suicide rates among jailed detainees are three times higher than they are among inmates in the prison population and over half of the jail suicides occur within the first week of incarceration.[2] Minnesota has eighty-two jails in eighty-seven counties, serving over 7,000 detainees.[3] The sheer gravity of these stats weighed on me, as did the FreeWriters mission I carried. That is to reach jailed detainees at a crucial time in their lives, in an environment that otherwise provides no emotional wellness programming or outdoor activities, while they await oft-delayed court dates.

The FreeWriters mindful writing practice is held in a classroom on the perimeter of the detainees' living quarters, which are called quads. Each quad has twenty electronically controlled cells that house two people. The detention officers' video control station is in the quad's center.

Attending a FreeWriters session is voluntary; most participants show up the first time just to break up the boredom of their listless routine. At first glance the detainees, clad in loose-fitting orange pajamas and plastic orange Crocs, appear indistinguishable—depersonalized. I make it a point to quickly learn their names. Newbies are mixed in with repeaters who know the system and routine. Repeaters hate county jail; they say prison has better food and more to do. Ninety percent of the attendees are people of color, which is perhaps not surprising, but is very discouraging. One in five Black people born in Minnesota in 2001 are likely to be incarcerated in their lifetimes, compared to one in ten Latinx people and one in twenty-nine white people.[4]

After a brief introduction about FreeWriters, I explain the mindful writing concept, and that we start out with a prompt. The prompt is the writing subject that launches a five-minute writing exercise. Examples are: *home, family, where I'm from, who I am, what I think, letters, jail, freedom, friend, ten years ago, ten years from now, choice, broken, do over, I'm going,* and *help*. Everyone writes using the same prompt.

Participants are allowed to write anything that comes to mind related to the prompt. If they can't think of anything to write, they are encouraged to simply keep the pencil moving, and more often than not, something will eventually come to mind. "Just let the writing do the writing. Spelling and grammar aren't important. Be honest. Be true to yourself." To begin the writers are asked to take a deep breath, be present, and write freely from a place where it's "safe to tell your story." At the end of five minutes, everyone is invited to read their writing out loud.

During a FreeWriters session, shortly after I started as an instructor, a detainee asked (more matter-of-fact than threatening), "So, tell me, what you got for me NOW? Something to help me on the street? You want me to pull a poem out my pocket up against a nine-millimeter Glock?" The other detainees laughed and waited to see my reaction.

There it was—the question that had been rolling around in my head from the start. I had a list of post-incarceration resources available including FreeWriters sessions held in a local church, free education, trade opportunities and addiction programs. But the question was, "What can you offer me now?" Not a week from now, or in a month, or when I get out, but right now?

It was an immediate question for me, and a urgent question for society at large. Many of us never really *see* incarcerated people. We're distracted by "get tough on crime" taglines or the bitter debate about the efficacy of social programs. In his book *The Caging of America*, Adam Gopnik points out that "currently, there are more Black men in the grip of the criminal justice system—in jail, prison, or probation—than were in slavery prior to the Civil War."

The author further contributes that we've "normalized the incarceration of people of color and turned it into an industry fed by those locked out of the mainstream and trapped within America's latest *caste* system."

The detainees stared at me blankly and waited for my answer. They didn't want some social theory; they wanted something actionable. I knew the therapeutic power of mindful writing, but in a transient jail setting, did it have legs?[5] What was the foundation, the underpinning, the secret sauce that soaked into your bones and propelled hope and fortitude going forward?

I felt trapped. The room spun and my throat went dry. Sweat sprang from my face and soaked my collar. The attendees were giving up on me and starting to talk amongst themselves. Then, I heard a word from somewhere within the chatter and spontaneously plucked it out.

"Honor," I said out loud.

The men looked at me curiously as I repeated the prompt. "Honor. You have five minutes; begin." To my surprise, their heads dropped and pencils raced across the page. I had no idea what to expect.

"Time's up, who wants to read?" I held my breath.

A hand went up. Interestingly, the participant was the detainee who had put forward the question I'd been unable to answer. As he read, his sparse words cracked open the siloed bravado of jail habitation that gives no quarter to vulnerability.

"I honor all the people who had my back—my two best friends shot down for nothin', my brother who don't think straight from getting hit in the head, my mother for working two jobs to get us through only to have me disappoint her, my grandfather who bought me football shoes that he couldn't afford. The homeless lady who slept in her car and gave me a ride to school every day. A cook at a fast-food place who tried to get me off drugs. I honor all the victims who've been pushed down and come right back up and help you. Honor all I got."

The room was silent, as if taking on the solemnity of a church.

Then, someone snapped their fingers . . . then another . . . then everyone, the snaps falling into synchronous rhythm, breaking off into claps.

I listened to the reader's words intently, aware that the man was helping me so we could better help each other. It was honor, yes, but not a flag-saluting tribute. This was honor, whose special context had eluded me but now filled me with gratitude. This was honor from the point of view of incarcerated people and their inherent struggle. Honor: The quality of having respectability, worthiness, a sense of hope and pride, and the ability to pick ourselves up no matter how many times we've fallen and carry on. Honor: The platform from which human beings can rise again for the benefit of themselves and others, on the street or wherever their journey takes them.

Other participants raised their hands, eager to read. With raw honesty and a sense of purpose, their fear, regret, loneliness, sadness, joy, and hope were laid bare for all to witness. Their words vibrated with the movement of life. They presented stories with amazing creativity, poetic rhythm, compassion, remorse, and humor. The stories and reflections were palpable; they cut to the bone and opened the heart. The stories taught the writers and informed all of us who cared to listen.

We (myself included) write on, breathe honor into the words, and become self-compassionate witnesses to our own stories. We take refuge in our writing from a place where the winds of worry have abated, the clouds of doubt and anger have cleared, and relief comes from knowing healing is accessible . . . now!

Footnotes:

1. Pennebaker, J. W., & Smyth, J. M. Opening up by writing it down: How expressive writing improves health and eases emotional pain. (2016).
2. Bureau of Justice Statistics: Survey of Inmates in Custody.
3. Vera Institute of Justice.
4. Department of Justice, National Institute of Corrections, 2019.
5. Zindel Segal, Distinguished Professor of Psychology, University of Toronto. *Mindfulness Based Cognitive Therapy (2013)*.

Reflection

Stephan Oseghale, FreeWriters Participant

Swimming is fun. It relieves stress and is great exercise. You know what else is fun? Floating. When you float, you give all your burdens to the water. You surrender. You trust the water to carry you gently. All you have to do is breathe, look up to the sky, and relax. Floating is an amazing feeling. It takes all your worries away and gives you a new sense of calmness.

That amazing feeling can be compared to how I felt every Wednesday at the FreeWriters class. It's not a therapy class. It's not an exclusive club with a fancy name. It was just a place I went to be myself. To express myself. A safe place. A place with no judgments. A place where I was free even though I was incarcerated.

You know, I always wondered why they called the class "FreeWriters." Like, why not "caged writers," "rough writers," "cuff writers," or some tough gangster name? Why FreeWriters? Why the word "free"? I was not free. I ate, slept, and took a shit in the same place. I was an inmate—a prisoner. I was not free.

I kept attending the class and I found the answer to my "why free?" question. Like an addict, I was chasing the good feeling—the floating experience I felt at the end of every class. I listened to the prompts from Nate and Melissa and I wrote. Over the course of months, I wrote my resentments away. I wrote my tears away. I wrote my fears away. I wrote my pain away. I became free.

By writing myself free, I was able to remove the blanket of self-pity and the scarf of sorrow I wrapped myself in. I began to learn new things about myself; I was reintroducing myself to myself. I learned how to organize my thoughts. By organizing what I think about, I'm able to organize my actions, which in turn will help organize my life. My life is not fully organized, as I am still in prison, but I am a work in progress.

Thanks to FreeWriters, I can forgive. I can love. I can trust and not hold grudges anymore. I also had the courage to seek professional help to talk about past traumatic experiences with a psychologist. Thank you Nate and Melissa, for encouraging me to write.

How to Read This Collection

Editor's Note

"Humankind has not woven the web of life.
We are but one thread within it.
Whatever we do to the web, we do to ourselves.
All things are bound together.
All things connect."

—*Chief Seattle*

Like the artist Jackson Pollock dripping paint on canvas, allowing art to take on a spontaneous life if its own, "mindful writing" similarly triggers a flash of unpredictable emotional expression on paper. The reveal may be trauma, addiction, moments of forgotten joy, a cry for help, a family crisis, gratitude, or remorse.

The five-minute writing exercise produces a mental release that frees the writer from being bound to past decisions and opens the door to charting a meaningful path forward.

Once released, many detainees attend weekly FreeWriters sessions held outside the jail. They credit the mindful writing practice with providing the support to journal, write their stories, compose lyrics, seek treatment, make amends, and further their education.

Some readers may read this collection in one sitting. Others may prefer to skip around and pick out "prompts" of particular interest. We suggest no pattern other than to take your time and set aside preconditioned notions related to incarcerated people. All of us have the power to recast our destiny if given the opportunity. This writing collection is like a sea of icebergs: Underneath these floating word islands is a jailed detainee, often forgotten, under duress, and struggling to survive in strained conditions with an uncertain future.

Finally, this collection is not just about jail detainees. Many people live in jails not made of concrete and steel doors, and they'll recognize the struggles presented here.

May these voices from jail bring you hope, healing, laughter, and insight and promote forgiveness. We can never be free until we are all free.

Illustration: *BESET* by S. Kilman, Arts from the Inside

Prompt One

I'm From

> I'm from poverty, molestation, addiction, violence and historical trauma. But it wasn't all bad. I'm from where resiliency and strength are bred, a place where courage is born and the will to not let where you're from define you.

The Hood

I'm from the hood, where we seem to be trapped, hurting one another, and stuck in the system we created ourselves. I'm from where selling rocks was the way to survive, until I picked up a rock and smoked it. Well, that damn rock consumed me mentally, physically, and emotionally, just like it did to everyone around me. I'm praying every day for a new start—a place where the sisterhood and brotherhood treat people how you want to be treated! In this new hood, love will outshine the bad. Kids will have a chance to grow up and be themselves. Is this new hood just a dream? Maybe. But dreams do come true.

Streets

I was born from a father with a good name in the community. I was always getting good grades in school. But somehow, I couldn't leave the streets alone, and that led me to years of jail time. Now, as I sit on the edge of my bunk, I ask myself, "Was it worth it?" Now people look at me differently. No matter. I need to start mattering to me.

Kings

I'm from
a father to a mother;
a past history of tribes;
a perfect harmony of music;
a powerful world of elements;
a street which I can live on;
a planet called Earth;
a unique set of faces;
a bloodline of kings.

Anonymous

I'd rather write about where I'm not from.
I'm not from a loving, kind, sheltering family.
My mother was too tired to spend time with me.

Lost

I can't find my way home.
I don't know what to do right now.
I don't know what to say.
I don't know how to feel.
I'm having mixed emotions;
everything's hitting me at once,
and it's overwhelming.
This writing does mellow out my mood;
it would, yeah.
I don't even know if I'll have an address to go home to.
Shit—I guess it's back to the halfway house.
Hopefully, I can get an address by Monday.
I'm so tired of the bullshit.
I got to do better . . . but shit happens.
I don't know. It is what it is. Tired of the B.S.

3 A.M.

That's where you'll find me when I'm out of jail. If you look around, you'll see individuals on the not-legit side of money-making. Either be a female bringing in money by selling herself or addicts everywhere trying to hustle one another or get over on one another. An occasional car drives by; it's either a cop car or someone looking for drugs. Me, I'm out this late usually to smoke a joint and get fresh air. Gotta watch your back.

Beauty

Where I'm from is what people in the suburbs call a dirty, dangerous place. Watch your step and avoid the needles on the ground. If kids don't know how to act, they wind up dead and on the news. Where I'm from, you might end up in the county jail fighting for your life just because you had to protect yourself. Where I'm from, the best food comes from the hood street stoves. Where I'm from is a place of unseen beauty. There's always beauty in the struggle.

Old School

I'm from a time when you caught fireflies in Mason jars,
and lay on your back and counted the stars.
I'm from, "Eat your veggies and do all your chores,"
to "Girls, help your mother at the store."
From, "Do as I say, not as I do,"
to, "Got no time for feeling blue."
From, "Stay on the porch when the sun goes down,"
to, "Guess what, y'all? Saturday cartoons are on."

Culture

Where I'm from, kids are ripped from their homes and placed in white schools that consist of priests and nuns who have one plan: to kill off the culture the children once lived by and to make them believe in God, for that is the only way to get to heaven.

Where I'm from, women neglect their babies and choose men over kids. They throw parties in the same home where they're supposed to protect these children.

Where I'm from, it's not uncommon to hear of grandma, auntie, sister, or foster homes raising my peers.

Where I'm from, my stepmom hates me because I remind her of my mom.

Where I'm from, my stepmom hates me because my dad loves me and I'm the baby.

Where I'm from, I'm the only girl, and therefore I'm left with lots of responsibilities.

Unknown

Where I'm from is a place where parents are drug addicts, from parents that were abusive. I'm from a state unknown to man, cuz sometimes I don't even know where I'm from. I'm from a place of no return, from a place that puts people in jail that have done nothing wrong. I'm from a place where it's cool to be a single parent. I'm from a place where violence is the norm. I am from a place where I was born to lose. I am from nowhere and everywhere at the same time. Where I am from is none of your fucking business.

No Doors

My place is my own
It's top secret, where the cover is not blown,
My place is safe, secure and sound
Everything within is bound,
My place is a place you don't want to be
Only because my place is what makes me, me,
Dare to enter my place if you must
It's a bond of love, anger and trust,
Respect my place as I respect yours
Do not try to knock as it has no doors.

Bottom Rung

I'm from here. Where else would a homeless person call home? When I had upscale friends, they might have said I was from money, finance and the high life. But I doubt they would answer to my name now, other than to call me out as a punch line at a cocktail party. "The guy that rode Jacob's ladder down to the bottom rung." If you were to ask my former wife where I'm from, she'd say, "Who Cares?" But if you insist, go ask my mother, she'll tell you I'm from Israel.

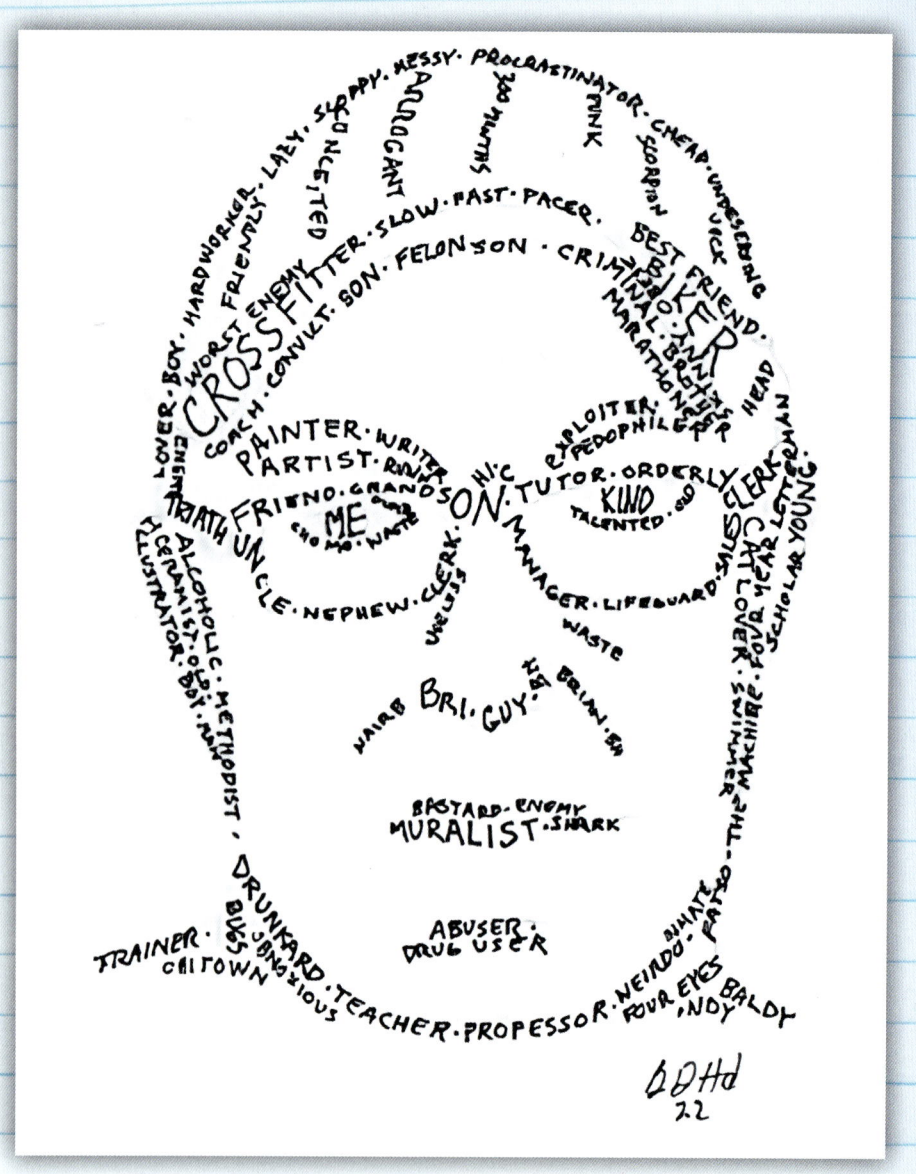

Illustration: *Self-Portrait of a Prisoner* by Brian Hindson, Justice Arts Coalition

Prompt Two

I Am
───

> I am a thinker, philosopher, tinkerer, socialist, realist, hard-worker, inventor, scientist, psychotic, alcoholic, drug-abusing danger to society. Mostly though, I am just lost.

Big Rig

I'm a trucker, a teamster. I've been driving since I was thirteen, when I made a go-cart out of an old lawnmower engine. At sixteen, I fixed up junkers and drove them in the demolition derby. Drove a delivery van and short-haul drayage before I did a stint in the Air Force as a mechanic.

When I got out, I had saved enough to put a downpayment on a used, fifth wheel Peterbilt with a sleeper cab. Running long haul was good until I stopped short of the I70 Eisenhower Tunnel to chain up in a snowstorm. I injured my back and ended up getting my spine fused, so I could walk and drive. But the pain never let up. You can't drive truck if you're on narcotics. This is where I made two mistakes at once. I bought pain killers at various truck stops and continued to drive my rig. It caught up to me. Running hot, on a rain-slicked, two-lane highway, coming into town, my truck jackknifed. The trailer swung into the oncoming lane and collided with a hotel shuttle bus.

Lot of people hurt. Wish it hadn't happened. Awful sorry about it. Now, everything has gone to shit. Dark. Lost my truck. Back pain won't let me sleep. I need meds, treatment. I'm circling the drain.

Divine

I wake up imprisoned in my mind
Hoping to find the great divine
Seeking a spiritual connection in its design
Living life not choosing crime
Knowing it's time for darkness to shine.

Don't Matter

Do I really matter to the rest? I know for me, I matter. I respect me. I acknowledge me. I love me. Shit, I don't give a fuck what the rest of them think. Motherfuckers don't matter to me, just like I don't matter to them. They all broke, homeless, and gang-bangin'. I'll never fit in with that crowd. I guess being a follower is the new trend. Yeah, they can keep that weak-minded shit.

Still the Man

If I could start from scratch, I'd probably say, "No thanks." My past has built me and chiseled me into the man I am today. Just because I'm in orange don't mean I am not a success. I just needed to be brought back to Earth, to a real place, to see what a gift my kids and my lady are.

I'm so thankful for them. Even with the problems I've caused, they still call me Daddy and Sweetheart. To them, I'm still the man. They are my past, my salvation, and I wouldn't change that, no matter what I look like to others. Starting from scratch comes with a lot of loss. I've had enough of that. I just want to hold on to what I have.

> 66

Good Kid

On the streets, I used to have nothing.
Turned into a hustler cuz I grew up struggling.
Mom's from Chicago, Dad's from New York,
I have the stock talk before I jumped off the porch.
People really don't know me.
I was a good kid; I crossed over like Kobe.
Used to rob just because I was greedy,
but I still gave away my pocket change.
In the streets, you could lose yourself to a nobody.
That's why I keep my head to the sky and let the Lord guide me.

If You Let Me

Whatever you think, I'm not my crime.
No matter where I am, my heart will shine.
You don't have to believe it because I know it's true;
even if you treat me poorly, I'll be kind to you.
God doesn't like ugly, so I pray for you.
Darkness in the heart will always come to light.
Only you can change yourself and make it right.
Not sure why it's so hard; you shouldn't put up a fight.
Let God's beauty shine through like the stars in the night.

Who

I am I—or am I you?
I am the thing you desire the most.
I am the thought that swims through your head,
the voice on your shoulder, and you are my host.
I am the one who plays tricks on your mind.
I am the one who convinces you to lie.
I am the one you will betray everyone for.
I am also the one who will watch you dying on the floor.

I am the one who brings you drama and pain.
I will also leave you stranded, stuck in the rain.
I will destroy your religion and steal your faith.
I am the demon, the darkness, the wraith.

I am I—or am I you?
Ask your addiction who is who?

Career

I started off as a bank teller at age sixteen, then moved on to be an accountant. Was I really living my dream? My dream was to become a lawyer, even as distant as it may seem. Through my blood, sweat, and tears, I know I will accomplish this. After all, it is my ultimate goal and dream.

Music

Music has shaped many aspects of my life. Mom was a music teacher. I was in a boys' choir traveling the world from age seven. I played/play many instruments and competed in many contests, singing and playing. Sometimes, I forget how simple music can be. The rhythm of the pencil on the paper could be considered music . . . footsteps down the hall . . . clanging cell doors. The sound of life, the Rhythm of Life. Music is joy, music is pain therapy. People with Alzheimer's cannot recognize their spouses or children, but they remember the jingle for their favorite cereal commercial from childhood. Music brings emotion you might not expect or want to feel. Ever think about soundtracks in movies? You didn't know the scene was sad until you heard the music. Music is a big part of my life. They can't take that away from me.

Friend

I am a man and a friend,
Who you can call when there's no end.
I am for the fam.
They need me, and there I am.
I am a Black man, so I have to work harder,
Cuz I grew up with no father; single mom had three daughters.
Oldest male in the house,
Shit no one ever taught us.
I am a Christian and slacking bad.
Birth Control has prevented me from being a dad.

Lamb

I Am the Blood, Sweat, and Tears
for All of the Years without the John Deeres.
I Am the Reality that gave History
a Story to tell in the Beginning.
I Am the Mystery to Nationality.
I Am the Reason for Proclamations and Emancipations;
I Am the True Declaration for Independence.
I Bear Witness that Abraham and Isaac Were Not Christians.
I Am the Vision, the Mozart, and Beethoven.
I Am the Chosen; I Am the Broken and Bruised.
I'm in all the Stories in Every City on Fox News.
I Am the Blues and the Jazz.
I Am the Good and the Bad.
I Am the First and the LAST.
I Am the LAMB, when you ask who I AM.

Hands

Beautiful, soft, long, sleek,
for cooking, folding, or striking a cheek.
Warm, calloused, old, slender,
great at rubbing, soothing, scolding, or being tender.
Short, young, brown, tan, white,
they can cook, speak, spank, and write.

Illustration: *Never Forget* by Zhi Kai H. Vanderford,
Justice Arts Coalition

Prompt Three

I Remember

> "
>
> I don't ever want to forget all the pain my addiction has caused me. I have been in jail so many times, one would think why haven't I learned my lesson by now? But that's the ugliness of this nasty disease... the deep dark places that it takes people to . . . I don't want to forget.

Rez Dogs

I remember living on the rez. We had nine dogs. To me, that was the shit because I liked to be outside and take nature walks. So, every day they would hear the back screen door open from a distance. Crazy, cause they would come from all directions. I didn't have to be afraid of walking the trails because the dogs were all around me, doing their own thing but also very aware. My oldest two, Bibbits and Worms, would stay close, and I would talk to them as if they could respond. But they actually listened to what I was saying. Bibbits would lie next to me on the porch if I was lying on the porch. Then, one day he just didn't come home . . . sad. Worms got beat with a two-by-four that had a nail stuck in the end. Stupid rez kids. You can never have anything good around them.

Other Me

I remember when I had my kiddos and life seemed so different. I lived in a condo with my grade-school boyfriend, who worked hard and then became a drug user. I was sober those days, thicker, long brown hair, no make-up or tan. Later in our relationship, upon getting preg again, I moved us into a town house. This is where I went to school, at Inver Hills. I worked my eight-hour job and took care of the house and the kids, although my relationship struggled, not only for me, but for my significant other, who took our boys' lives. This when everything became what it is today. I've had good and bad experiences, but I miss my other me and old life.

I Forgot

I forgot my age so many times. I forgot how I have been loved so many times. I forgot how it feels to be loved. I forgot how to love somebody as much as they love me. I forgot all the pain my parents gave me. I forgot all the lies I was told. I forgot that you are not loved by someone who abuses you. I forgot that abuse can be verbal, spiritual, physical, and sexual. I forgot that ABUSE IS NOT LOVE. I forgot how many times you think you are in love, and you can still be proven this love is not for real. I forgot to forget all my shortcomings and move on with my life and to forgive myself and others.

Children

If I could go back in time, I'd go back to when I first took a drink, or maybe that moment in my young adult life that made me the addict I am today, and try to stop it from happening. But I'm more interested and hopeful for my children's future. I desperately care about their lives and want to see that they could be more than I ever was. To see, hopefully, that I didn't fuck them up too bad. From where I am now, I can't even change my baby's diaper. It's probably best—while my intentions are good, I don't yet trust myself.

When I Was a Girl

When I was a girl, I cried once.
I was lost inside a foster home,
wrapped up like a bug in a rug
inside my own clutter, not in touch
with anything I was familiar with.

When I was a girl, my period came
while I was in Isanti Girls' Ranch.
Where the hell was Mom when
I was waking up in a system
breeding me for the penitentiary,
in a lake of blood, hoping for love?

How did you get loved when you were a girl?
Can't tell me much? Yeah, toxic shame isn't a game.
Now, all eight of us kids are trying to raise our kids,
only not giving enough.
Is it us or from when we were girls?
Let's talk.

First Sip

I remember when life was so easy, carefree, and fun. This was when I was a child, up until age fourteen. Age fourteen is when I first started my addiction. I remember when I had that first sip of beer. I hated it, but my sister made me finish it. After that first beer was gone, I knew I had arrived and was in love. I have battled my addiction now for more than half of my life.

Dad

I remember my dad was on my side.
Every time I lost him, I ended up here.
I wish I could bring him back.
RIP, Dad.

Hard Lessons

I can remember my first hard lesson. How can I forget?
I was locked in a closet with an empty box of Ritz Crackers
for two hours—maybe longer, maybe shorter.
How could I know? I was only five years old.
I remember sitting there, asking myself what was so wrong
with sayin', "Mom, I'm hungry," and, "Pick me up."
But I guess everything was wrong.
'Cause my little hand was still bandaged up from when
she stuck it on top of the hot burner on the stove.
Yeah, I guess I've had a few hard lessons.

Legacy

my name, my dignity, my heart, my ambition, my reputation,
my honesty, my class, my children, my mistakes, my failures,
my milestones, my accomplishments, my weaknesses, my flaws,
my light, my wisdom, my generosity, my honor, my integrity,
my wealth, my worth, my thoughts, my intuitiveness, my vision,
my insight, my intelligence, my authenticity.

Illustration: *All in One* by Roberto Lopez-Rios,
Arts from the Inside

Prompt Four

Jail

> Pain is heavy or light depending on who you share it with. Right now, locked down, I'm alone and I'm suffering. Please let me know you're there for me.

Fork

My orange pajamas are soaked from sweat that has pooled in the crackling, vinyl-covered, mattress. It smells of piss. A torturous, tick, tick, tick, randomly emanates from the closed ventilation panel on the ceiling. I can't breathe. A tension headache, from an unseen hand, squeezes my oxygen-depraved sawdust brain. If I had a fork, I'd stick it in my neck. Instead, my thoughts turn to twisting my clothes into a rope, but I can't find an overhead purchase to secure a noose. I turn to the gray wall and work my fingers into the concrete pock marks. Each indentation a star—part of a constellation in the expansive, celestial universe. I'm Icarus, a terrestrial traveler, seeking the radiant healing of the sun, careful not to get burned again.

Touch

My hands feel tied. I feel like I have so much to do, but I'm stuck here and can't help myself. Everything in my life is under someone else's control—in their hands. My hands need to feel loved ones. I need to feel my grandchildren, children, and parents, but mostly my significant other. My hands feel empty and alone, and it makes my heart hurt waiting for them to feel again. My hands play a huge role in everything I'm going through. I'm tired; I'm empty; I want to fix everything.

What I Want

What I want is to get out of jail.
What I want is to make bail.
What I want is not so much to ask.
All I want is a treatment pass.
What I want is to stay free.
What I want is to make life a breeze.
What I want is not so much to ask.
What I want is not an easy task.
All I need is my kids and no drugs.
So, I'm pretty sure I need to stop dating thugs!

Concoctions

I miss my own cooking. These trays give my stomach anxiety. They say good food is made with love. Well, these jailhouse meals, I just hate 'em. Same stuff three times. Maybe twice a week some are okay. To get one extra item, you pay. I miss opening the refrigerator and having options. Instead, we get the roll-of-the-dice concoctions. Soul food, Cup Food, fast food—all beat no food except jail food.

Saved

Being behind these walls has saved me from tragedy.
I feel depression pulling me down like gravity.
I'm just watching time pass away and family's mad at me.
Court date too far away; can't pay the ransom fee.
Still alive, so hey, I'm blessed to be.
To some this is hell; I agree,
but who put me in this situation? Only me.

Cage

Like a rat in a wire wheel, a cage made of steel.
Round and round we go; pain I still feel.
Names and faces subject to change,
but seems the machine stays all the same.

In The Moment

In the heat of the moment, I made a decision to turn myself in. After being on the run for two years, I was tired of being rejected for places to rent because of my background, so I made a change. In the heat of the moment, I called the police and told 'em to pick me up. I have a warrant and a felony; now I'm here, facing the consequences of my actions. Maybe it's a good thing, maybe bad, or maybe just stupid. Now that moment is gone and all I feel is cold.

Dreams

Trapped inside concrete walls, on a metal bed frame with a mat and no pillows.
Ice cold everywhere you touch . . . No cuddles allowed.
I hate to wake up in the morning and face the reality outside of my dreams.
Dreaming of being outdoors, at home with loved ones, and free.
They won't let me sleep; gotta wake up to nowhere.
They try to kill your hopes and dreams; they hate it when you boast.
They don't want you to feel comfort, happiness, love, or hope.

Stress

weird-ass dudes, cornballs, locked doors, P.O., nasty-ass food, liars,
boredom, no structure, lockdowns, rudeness, body odors, snitches, bitches,
judgmental people, being a light-skinned Black man, can't go home, expensive phone calls.

Closed Heart

It is very sad that the County Jail makes so much money but cannot provide heat.

It's bad enough that I've been frostbitten, and anytime it gets cold enough I suffer from pain.

My freedom is already taken; I shouldn't have to suffer. I'm here for protecting myself from a man who violated me while I was sleeping. We all need justice. It's not fair we don't have our freedom and are also stuck under lights almost twenty-four hours a day!

Beautiful Day

Today is a beautiful day—
in here, out there, cold or not.
I can't see it or feel it, but I know in my heart that today is a
    beautiful day—
a day to heal hurts, and win personal wars in all kinds of ways.
Today is a beautiful day in every single kind of way.
Sunrise, mid-day, sunset, twilight, Halley's comet.
Hey! What a beautiful day!

Pod 7A

It's jail. I'm ready to go. I never, ever wanna hear about Pod 7A ever again. I pray for all the women in Pod 7A and for those to come. We're really just passing through. It's time to finish living our lives and let this be a distant memory and a lesson learned for each of us. They can't hold us forever. So, I hope each lady gets through this, and remember, we all make mistakes. As long as we endure this, as the Bible says, "This too shall pass."

23 & 1

Damn, 23 & 1 has been a routine in my life since I was twelve years old. 23 & 1 means coming out only one hour a day and being on lockdown twenty-three hours a day. I experienced 23 & 1 in Redwing, Stillwater, Rush City, St. Cloud, Lino Lakes, and Faribault prisons. I am not a fuck-up, and I know how to adjust to my surroundings. Twenty-three & 1 brings a lot of humility to my life. 23 & 1, oddly enough, has been a good learning experience.

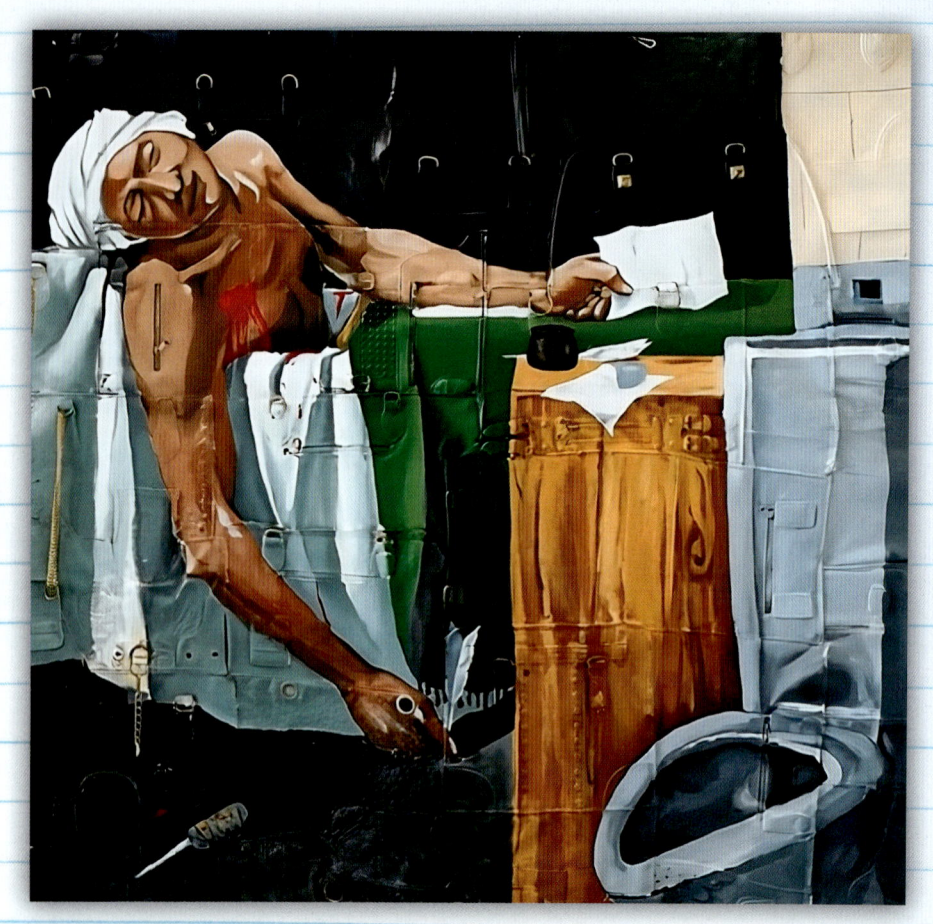

Illustration: *Three is a Crowd* by Russell Craig,
The Right of Return Fellowship

Prompt Five

Letters

___

> I'm writing to let you know that I'm in jail. I might need your support and I will let you know when I do. Support for my thoughts and feelings. I don't know what I can tell you right now, I think the jail keepers read every letter.

❝

Cursive

I waited like a dog on a bone for her letters and sniffed them out, hoping to catch her scent. I slow-played the opening, keeping them away from the snoopy perps in my quad. In my cage, I unfolded the crisp, velum paper and absorbed her cursive loops that flow across the page like a musical score. I searched for traces of what she was doing in the moment . . . a coffee stain, a lock of hair, maybe a makeup smear. She kept me informed about her college scene, our mutual friends, her dog, and the love songs that connected us. I wrote too . . . about how much I missed her and future plans. I promised to do better. Careful not to let the pencil slip off into reality . . . as in, my stay in isolation for a fight I didn't start, or that I have a swollen black eye, or that I spent two days in a suicide vest. I kept her every letter. When my sentence came down, the letters stopped coming. Now, I just read the old ones, play our love songs in my head, and cry.

Ask Me

Write me a letter and ask me how I feel.
Ask me how I am; ask me anything, everything.
By asking, I won't feel so all alone.
By asking me, I'll feel as though someone cares—
like I'm worthy of attention and my opinion matters.
Right now, I need people to help me; I waste away in jail.
So please, ask me anything, and I will do my best to help you too.

Self

Dear Michael, when you go home in a month, make the best of yourself and life to better your future. Spend the time with your kids and woman. You've missed them so much these fifty days away. Just take the time to show them how much you care. A text can be erased; spoken words can go in one ear and out the other, but a letter saved in your heart is forever.

Pickled

Hey brother, sorry I worried you. I know they told you I was under a suicide watch after I got arrested. I was so effing wasted, full of shame and freaked out, I can only recall fragments of those first couple of days in lock down. Except for the pickle suit, that's an experience I'll never forget. They wrapped me naked in this sleeveless gown that was made of hard plastic on the outside with an itchy quilted fabric on the inside that smelled like piss. They said it was for my own protection cause it's impossible to make a noose out of it. The guys in here call it a pickle suit cause it's green. They also say its what they make the terrorists in Gitmo wear. I don't know if I was trying to kill myself or not. But I was in a dark place, still am, just not as dark. Maybe this is the rock bottom I needed.

In Touch

I want to get in touch with my friend Leah. When I was six years old, I ran to her house to get in touch with the police because my mom and dad were trying to kill each other. When I was fourteen years old, Leah got in touch with me, said she couldn't do it anymore. I was confused, didn't know what she meant. Then her mother got in touch with me. Told me she had found Leah hanging in her closet—the very closet she hid me in when my parents came looking for me. The very place I had run to get in touch with some kind of normalcy.

Face-to-Face

Screw texting, never call, but I won't write a letter either.
I'd rather communicate face-to-face, which I don't do so well neither.
I'm kinda shy. Oh well, at least I'm not a biter.
Come in my cell if you wanna find out if I'm a fighter.
I'm depressively bipolar. Some days I'm warm and blowing up your phone.
Others, I'm colder and won't leave home.
But no matter how upset I get, I know I'm never alone.
That's why I love you, Jesus.

Open Letter

What are you all saying about me? That I'm an animal, a beast, a danger to society, a being without morals, a soulless individual, a bastard child, a waste of resources, the face of liberal policies. That I should be denied bail, locked down and flushed out of society. Maybe so. But I don't' really give a fuck about what you think because you don't know me. You only know stereo types, media hash, crime reports, isolated incidents and the political red meat you dine on. But if you got close enough to unpack my childhood, the layers of abuse, trauma and survival choices, you might find your heart and mine.

Better Late

Better late than never to write as if it's your last.
Or, go ahead—if you got love for a certain lady, write that lass.
Better late than never for politics to change on marijuana.
Ain't nobody getting beat up, not even for a dollah.
Weed only illegal if you some kinda street hustla.
I'm just on my own, trolling a little ganja.
Better late than never for my public defender.
I just want her to stop being a pretender.
At least come with your false hope.
This ain't no turn and burn joke.

To My Twelve-Year-Old Self

I used to say the words that
    would hurt someone's soul.
Because my heart was hurting,
    I wanted others to hurt too.

I wanted to pull back the curtain
    from my pent-up darkness.
I just wanted someone to help
    me in my fight for light.
My shoulders were so tiny and
    I was so young.
I did the best I could,
    even though I was lost and lonely.

So, to my twelve-year-old self:
    You did alright.
I'm proud of you—and you made
    it thru alright.

For You

I hope this letter finds you well.
I hope the sun is at your back and the path clear before you.
I hope your pain is contained and your struggles bearable.
I hope you forgive me for everything I fucked up for you.
If I had known now what you know, then maybe I would have done things differently.
I hope the best for you. You deserve it.
Love Always, You.

Passages

I'll be there when you open your eyes, baby girl.
I'll be there when you fall.
I'll be there when you get your first kiss.
I'll be there when you graduate.
I'm sorry, baby girl, I'm not there now.
I hate the situation I'm in.
When I get out, I'll never leave you.

Stunned

I wanted you to hear this from me, so you know the truth about what went down. The day I got shot in South Minneapolis, I was with my friend in a parked car, chillin. When out of nowhere, some guys with guns surrounded us. They opened the car doors and told us to give them the money. We refused. I had $5K under my sweater and a gun under my leg that they didn't know about. They made my friend get out of the car and started to search him. When I turned to look at the dude who was covering me, he hit me in the face with his gun and it went off. Everyone was stunned. I couldn't hear. The smell of gunpowder and a blue haze filled the car. I thought I was shot in the face. My friend took off running. I tried to get out of the car. The dude who hit me with the gun grabbed me from behind. I took my gun off safety and pointed it behind me and shot. It was a near miss to his head. We kept tussling and fell to the ground. His homies started shooting at me with an AR pistol and hit me three times then took off. I tried to get up but kept falling, leaving a trail of blood in the snow. I'd been shot in both legs but managed to stumble to a house, where someone called an ambulance. I'm patched up and in jail, but no worries, I'm good. Love you.

Illustration: *Sorrow of The Soul* by Kenneth Reams, Justice Arts Coalition

Prompt Six

Broken

> If stress is a killer, then I'm walking dead. Now I constantly need to be doped up so I can function without being paranoid. PTSD is a motherfucker. Anxiety, tension, irritability, without help, it's all gonna boil over someday.

❞

Recommend

I wish I had a high school experience. Instead, I had juvenile prison, a working ranch, and a shitload of mental health issues. Oh, and can't forget about the emotionally abusive therapist. Ug! After that, I dropped out of high school at seventeen with only two-and-a-half credits to get my diploma. But hey, would I rather go to class or get high? Guess which path I chose? See, I can't tell anyone what to do, but I'd highly recommend you don't do any of the shit I did.

Shattered

Broken, Broken, Broken. . .
This word impacts me a lot.
You see, I'm a Broken Fucking Human,
but I don't give that a second thought.

Everything I know is broken—
shattered like fractured glass.
But it all somehow fits together;
in a way that's a total pain in the ass.

But you may wonder what about me is broken?
Well, it's everything—mind . . . body . . . and soul.
I'd do anything to fill those gaps,
anything to fill that hole.

Plank

Walk the plank and don't look down.
Keep your balance or you'll hit ground.

Here comes a distraction to make you fall.
It can be love, friends or a free for all.

Each step will bring you closer to the end.
Have faith in what's around the bend.

Walk the plank and don't look down.
Snap. Crackle. Pop. I'm holding my ground.

Trust

Why should I trust you after all you put me through?
You led me into a dark cave and open grave of misery.
You were always sending me somewhere that had offended me.
Now, I have the space and opportunity to leave you.
So why should I trust you when everything about you is brand new?
I would be a damn fool to follow you around with my head on the ground.
You take my smiles and turn them into frowns.
Watch out. Watch out.

Freedom

Freedom comes with sobriety and recovery. Freedom is when I finally make it to Teen Challenge. Freedom isn't just physical. Freedom, for me, comes from the inside. Freedom comes with my thoughts—freedom from the negative attitude and self-defeating thoughts. Freedom in jail is when we come to group here at FreeWriters with equally growth-minded peers. Freedom is when I'm in sobriety and recovery.

Restless

I feel restless when I have nowhere to go.
I feel restless when I miss my mom and dad.
I know it's been hard on them, me getting kicked out of school and suspended.
I feel bad about everything I did.
I feel sad when I don't have anywhere to go.
Sometimes, I feel like the only person I can lean my head on is my girlfriend.
It is very hard being locked in a cell all alone.
I wish I could give my mom a hug.

My Story

In my twenty years, I've been violated, discriminated against, and suffered in abundance. The same people who are scared to say it to my face—instead, talking shit to their group of friends—have no idea about my trials and tribulations. It's cool though. Fuck 'em. I've been saying that, "fuck 'em," since I was a five-year-old boy being molested by my fourteen-year-old foster brother. I've said "fuck you" to the people who caused my scars, whether physical, mental, or emotional. I go by the name Mufasa on the street, but maybe I should change it to Scar. I wish I still had my momma in my life, but that's wishful thinking because she died when I was eighteen months old, and my dad was never around with his bitch ass. Bitch ass nigga was so scared of jail, the same place I am now, that he blew his brains out. I'm braver than my dad—more of a man.

Fentanyl

Came in like a storm with no shelter—
like a volcano on a small, crowded island.
It struck when I was 14 at the Broadway McDonald's.
It's a storm that took away people close to me.
I hope we find a way out of this storm.
It can blow anyone away.

❝

Delay-Delay-Delay

I try to make amends and they rip my life off instead. I agreed to a plea deal so I could get back to my job, pay my rent, and child support. My public defender said she'd have me out in ten days. I called my boss at the auto parts store, where I'm a manager, about the situation. He said, he'd hold my job. At my hearing, I'm told that my case has been delayed as my public defender, unfortunately, no longer works for the county. I'm being assigned a new PD. Ever since, it's been DELAY – DELAY – DELAY! I've been in this shit hole for over 90 days now. My boss gave up on me and I lost my job. I'm being evicted from my apartment and my ex has lawyered up about child support. I'm shouting for some justice but no-one hears me – all I get back is an echo of anger, rage and depression.

Older

Broken hearts, broken promises, broken bones . . .
I've broken homes, broken phones and
been broke and alone.
But now I'm older,
and I must be the handyman of my life,
so I won't be broke no more.

Escape

I feel like shit. When I first arrived at the Hennepin County Jail for booking, I knew I didn't have enough fetty in my system to last the night. So, naturally, I began to think about an escape route out of this hell hole. My number one plan was to let them know I overdosed, thinking that they'd have to take me to the hospital and from there, I'd escape and be back on the streets. Well, that plan backfired big time. To teach me a lesson they left me in booking for two days before bringing me up into the jail. I sat caged in isolation for what I think was a week and sweated out the most torturous withdrawal's imaginable.

Bounty Hunter

After running less than one hundred feet, out my back door, from a bullshit bounty hunter, not wanting to get shot or tazed, I laid down on my stomach in the gravelly dirt, my heart pounding. I could hear my daughter screaming, being held back, and felt the hot iron of trauma brand her being. Roughly handcuffed and pushed into the back seat of this fake cop's car, I pressed my face against the closed window and shouted, "I love you, be strong." As we drove off, I threw-up in that prick, bounty hunter's, back seat.

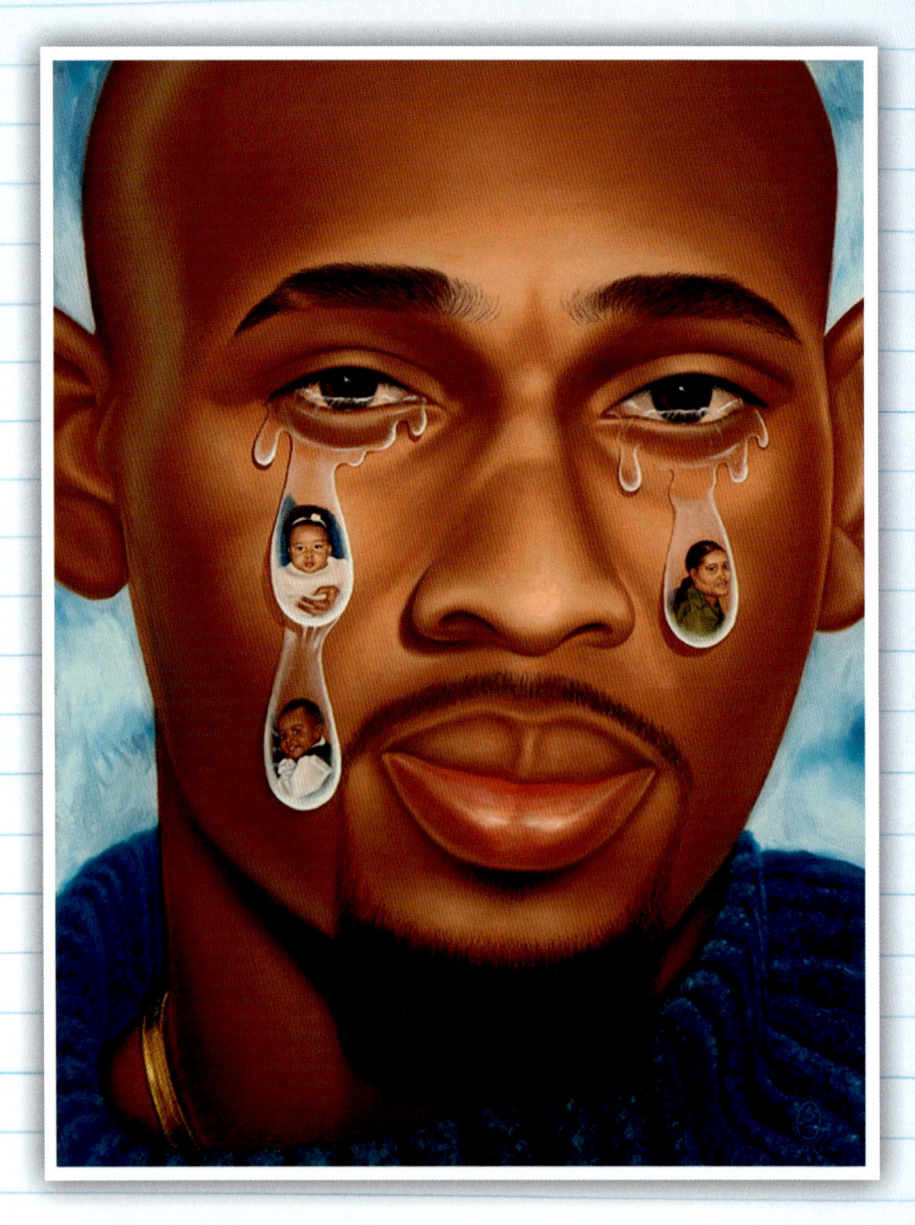

Illustration: *Eric Reese Tear Drop* by Fulton Leroy Washington, Arts By Wash

Prompt Seven
Forgiveness

> I own what I've done and don't expect the people I love to forgive me. I can't forgive me either. The only thing holding me together are my brothers in orange. They get where I'm at. That's all I've got right now.

The Judge

Do I deserve to be forgiven? There were times when I was asked to forgive someone and I didn't. I couldn't . . . wouldn't. Figure it wasn't my place to make that decision. Now, the judge won't look past my indiscretions and forgive me. My ex acts like she can't forgive me. Hell, my kids are missing valuable time with me as we speak—time I can't give back. Will they forgive me when it's all said and done? Can I ask for something I withheld from others?

Making Sense

Do we ever really forgive? Is it really, truly possible? I tend to think it depends on the amount of pain one has had to endure. I wonder to myself how it is that I can forgive a man who shot me, put me close to death, and caused me so much physical pain, but yet I struggle to truly forgive a woman who scorned me and caused me tremendous emotional pain. How does that begin to make sense? Is it because I trusted the woman with my most sacred possessions, like my heart and my life? I never trusted the man with a damn thing. But somehow, I just can't wrap my head around the idea.

Why We're Here

Why are we here? Well, I'm here because I've been greedy in life and don't know when to stop taking shortcuts. Decisions and communication—I've cut corners a lot. I'm a ruin of my life. I tend to not be grateful for what I have until it's too late. Forgive me. Now that I'm here, I've learned a lot about gratitude, and the little things in life I've grown to appreciate.

When I Said "No"

I really didn't mean it.
I'm sorry, Mama.
I wasn't there with you when you were all alone at the hospital.
The moment I got the phone call from the hospital, I wish I
    could have been there with you
 . . . and not on house arrest.
I'm sorry, mama; I wasn't there to hold your hand tight
 . . . until you took your last breath, the day you passed.
I'm so, so, so, so sorry Mama!
I love you!!!!

Courage

Hey, unborn, have the courage to come out of the womb.
Have the courage to face this unfamiliar world.

For lack of courage daddy let you down.
I didn't have the courage to stick around.

I hope it ain't to late, cause I have courage now,
to fight,
no matter the strife,
to be part of your life.

Don't worry. Have courage.

It's going to be alright.
One day we'll be so tight.

Could It Be?

Could it be that I've
learned how to pray?
That I could be forgiven?
Received another chance
in life?
In court?
For my children?
To be released February 9th?

Thanksgiving

It's hard to think about Thanksgiving five years from now. I don't know whether I'll be next to my child or eating with the brothers in the prison chow hall.

Thanksgiving is the day my ancestors got robbed, given blankets infected with smallpox and given liquor, knowing that shit's rough. Now, it's most Native Americans' downfall.

Thanksgiving is four days after my birthday. I'll be thirty-five. I just pray I'll be alive because lung and brain cancer is a strain that genetically runs through my veins.

Luck

Luck sucks
I believe in blessings.
I'm blessed to still be here
I ain't second-guessing.

Every day I thank god
I got in with a good mod.

Even tho y'all is cool
I can't wait to get out and take my son to school.

I'm glad I came to this class and said "hey"
I hope you guys have a blessed day.

Meds

Meds keep me going straight ahead.
I slam 'em so I can get to bed.
Got a brain full of worry and dread;
gotta stoke my pain with street meds.
If you in my way, I'd run ya over,
then bob and weave for cover.
If I hurt you, please forgive me.
I'm so full of suffering, I can't see.
Don't know about tomorrow's plight;
just trying to make it through the night.

Anger

Anger is a secondary emotion that most people aren't aware of. Anger is what you feel after you feel embarrassed, shammed or threatened. But once you learn to control anger, recognize it, channel it, life changes for you. But no matter how much I know about anger, I seem to be addicted to it, the adrenaline rush, the violence. But I hate the consequences, like jail, broken relationships, or hurt feelings. Sorry about that. My anger lies dormant inside of me. People look at me and don't see it, but I promise you, there is a thin line between my smile and the anger inside me. Wish it wasn't so.

Different

We all are of a different size, appearance and personality.
We all have different views, beliefs and languages, yet many similarities.
We all judge others, sometime harshly, sometimes with kindness.
We all love, hate, seek acceptance and want to be recognized.
We all eat, breathe, cry, laugh and bleed.
We all are somebody's child.
We all feel hurt and struggle.
We all crave affection.
We all have insecurities and make mistakes.
We all have it within our hearts to be accepting and considerate.
Why then do we not extend our love and forgiveness to the incarcerated?

Illustration: *Self Portrait* by Kenneth Reams, Justice Arts Coalition

Prompt Eight
Choice

> People say I'm smart, yet here I am. My grandfather, my father, my brothers, my cousins all deal on the street. It's the family business. I don't know what to do. I'm scared.

Resolution

I'm in jail, but my goal is to get out of jail without any ding to my record, so I can go back to work to take care of my sons and be a good citizen. I'll exercise every day and do my rituals to radiate love, joy, and happiness to the ones around me and to the world. I can create heaven on Earth for my family and work with influencers to create the next generation of human beings with love, joy, and happiness.

Freedom

Today's choices are tomorrow's reality!
Freedom isn't just about incarceration because there's many
    incarcerated who are mentally free.
Freedom is all about being—being able to express, live, and
    make decisions.
One can be free physically, but trapped mentally and emotionally.
In order to truly experience the inner peace and tranquility that
    comes from freedom,
one must be open to all the possibilities of a new existence and
    be able to let go of things
that have held them confined to a certain place or situation.
Only then, can the realm of freedom become a reality.

Same Old

Gonna stop doing the same old shit. But I like doing the same old shit. Maybe just change the shit that gets me locked up. I love doing most of the stuff that got me locked up, but maybe I should start doing the things I used to do before drinking. Bring back the good hobbies. Make more time for my kids and not be so selfish. Give back to the community. Might make a difference and not have so many young men and women making the same mistakes I made, and worse. Can't change the world if I don't start somewhere. Like Mike said, "I'm starting with the man in the mirror."

What If?

What if I was to actually do as I want and beat addiction? Just think how happy and fulfilled I would be. Life would have meaning to me, rather than just everyone else telling me how much my life is worth. I really hope I'm strong enough to make the change. I look forward to a better life. I would like to be on the other side of the Women in Orange and help them want to see change in their lives as well.

This Life

This life is not the life I thought I'd be living.
This life was supposed to be filled with joy, no pain.
This life seems unfair. Fucking bullshit.
This life seems very fair. Incredible wonders.
This life still has potential, even when I don't want to live it.
Why do I have to go on suffering?
I'd really like to skip the shitty parts of my life.
Lessons. Blessings. Disciplinary Actions. Consequences.
This life will be worth it, eventually, I hope.
For the sake of my girls, I won't give up on this life.
At times I want to.
Constant battles with an inner demon suck.

No Tears

A great day for me is waking up with no worries on my mind or heart and being able to feel the loss of my brother and boyfriend without crying every time I think of them. Being able to help people without the feeling I am being taken advantage of and being able to spend time with myself knowing everything is going to be all right.

Goals

My goal is to be positive and happy. I've learned in recovery that less is more, and I don't need, need, need. I have all I need. My goals are to get married, have children, go to church, become a nurse, stay sober, and be the best wife and mother I can be. I'd have two pit bulls and live in the suburbs with enough backyard for the dogs and kiddos. A pool would be nice to get that vitamin D I'm used to from being a Florida baby. My goal is to also to make it to Fiji one day.

Don't Ask Me

Don't ask me to do more drugs.
Please don't ask me to do more bad things.
This life is rough already, and I know it.
Don't ask me to do more damage to myself.
I know what's right, but don't ask me to go right.
I always wanted to, but I always go left when I know what's right.

Release

I want more than anything to get released. Today, I've been praying and putting God first, and I hope it's in his plan for me to go home. I want to go home to my brand-new apartment that I have yet to unpack, slow down, and soak in the fact I've come this far. I'm seven months sober, and there were days I didn't think that would even be possible. I wanna get back to living. I wanna get happy and sober, remember every detail of my life, and go back to my family and friends.

Stop

This jail stuff isn't for me,
The drugs aren't for me,
Why do I choose these things for me?
Without this stuff I'd have everything for me,
Sobriety, my kids, a home, a family,
How do I stop doing this shit that's not for me?

Chase

There is nothing that I chase as relentlessly as escape from this reality. I find it all sorts of places: the bottom of a bottle, the end of a pipe, the pages in a book, and the world of TV shows. I'll do anything as long as it gets me out of my own fucking head and this concrete hell. I used to chase people, but I got burnt too many times, so I won't do that again.

Ride

This is what I want in life: I want to be with my horses out in Cali. I want to brush them clean and put boots on their front feet for riding. Then, I want to put the saddle pad on with the saddle and fasten the girth. Then put my helmet on with my bridle and get on and ride. Take me to the Hollywood hills and show me all the beautiful things life has to offer.

Illustration: *Breast Milk* by Fulton Leroy Washington, Arts By Wash

Prompt Nine

Family

> The sadness and guilt of not being with my family is crushing me. I tell my kids not to worry, mommy will be home soon. To make that happen, I gotta stay sober and get my head straight. I'm working on it.

Visitors

When I was in the county can, before COVID, we'd get in-person visitors. Mostly, my mom would visit. She'd take the bus if the weather was okay. The visiting room was a closet-sized concrete cube with a glass partition. No touching. I hated it. All my mom did was cry, and like me, she had no escape. We both left the twenty-minute session feeling worse for the visit. I'm now back in county, the dumb shit that I am, and there are no more live visitations; it's all remote on a Zoom-type service. It costs my mom four bucks a session. It's so weird watching, from a distance, the collective dysfunction of my family on full display. I can see my mother's health deteriorating as she blows smoke rings at the screen. My crackhead sister shouts insults at me over my mother's shoulder. My brother floats in and out of the screen like a ghost, as my mother goes on and on about his abusive behavior and the recent restraining order filed against him. She wants me to knock some sense into him. In jail, my world has stood still and the sober isolation has cleared my head. My family is like a TV show with a bad script and weak plot; I can see what's coming as they bounce off the guard-rails, ignore the danger signs, and head toward the cliff. I no longer want to take that ride.

Burden

You should have told me that I was a burden to you before you realized that the burden of me has made you hate me.

You should have told me that I could not have any of your cigarettes instead of to "suck it like a straw" . . . because I was three years old.

You should have told me that someday you wouldn't be able to talk to me because there would be cancer in your brain, and still addiction in your heart.

You should have told me to be a better mother to my kids.

You should have told me that they would get old fast and that I would too.

You should have told me that I would turn into you.

Success

What I want is to come so far in my recovery that all I smell is success. Being a paralegal is my career goal. Hugging my children and family is all I want and know. I love them; they stand by me during my toughest times. Family really means the world to me, and I'm blessed to still have that. I love you all so much!

Holding It In

Since I was eight years old, I've been holding it in—
all these built-up emotions, built up anger.
Now, look what type of place I'm in.
If only my mom had asked me,
after I took care of my dying pops for all them years,
about how I felt or my state of mind. Fuck!
Bet I'll call my kids every day;
ask them what's on their minds and hearts,
so they ain't Holding It In.

Pieces

I can honestly say, for as long as I can remember, I was the one who would BE THERE for anyone for anything! It started with my parents. I was always there for my brother and sister, six and twelve years old. I was a mother and father to them until I was sixteen years old and had to move out on my own because I had to learn to live on my own and make my parents be the parents they should have been. I was tired of always being there to pick up the BROKEN PIECES OF THEIR ALCOHOLIC HOME. It was time for them to be there!

>

The Day I Was Born

The day I was born was the day my life of shit started. My childhood was rough; my mom and dad split young. At five years old, I had reconstructive eye surgery from my mom's boyfriend punching me in the face so much. I used to go to school and get made fun of, then come home and watch my mom's boyfriend beat my mom and us kids. I would do whatever I could to get my mom's boyfriend to hit me instead of my siblings. I did what I could. A couple years ago at a Fourth of July gathering, my brothers and sisters broke down drunk and asked me how I felt as an abused kid. The truth is I just made sure they were okay. It turned me into a monster for a long time, but today I can humbly say I am a child of God, full of love.

Feet Forward

Walking in the sand—behind me, my son jumps into my
    barefoot impressions.
My daughter carries a pail and shovel toward the water—my
    angels just enjoying life again.
Soon, I will be there to hold you when the sand gets too hot.
I'll walk in God's impressions, so that I walk on the right path.
Forward I'll walk, as backward is no longer an option.

Why

I had a lot of anger growing up and remember going into the hospital when I was younger for my uncontrollable rage. I don't understand why my birth mother drank so much while I was in her stomach. It pretty much messed up my brain from the start, right up to this day. I'm still learning how to control anger. I know being adopted hurt me. They didn't want to deal with my issues and gave me up to the foster care system. I hated it and I hate jail.

Grandma

This year brought me my first grandson, whom I still haven't met, but hopefully, by mid-year I will be introduced to him. It's sad because I don't even know his name. I have been incarcerated and my son has cut off all communication with me. His wife, who I used to talk to, also cut off communication with me after I asked to be in the hospital when she went into labor. I'm guessing my son told her to block me because his father has brainwashed him into believing I'm not worthy of being his mother and that his wife, my son's stepmother, should be called "Mom," and now, I'm sure, "Grandma." Even though I raised my son by myself, his entire life.

Help

I want to work on my addiction. I've been on a binge for a while that is wearing and tearing me down. I need more people to advocate for me. I know recovery takes time. I can't say where I'll be five years from now; hopefully not prison. I gave my kids up. I beat myself up a lot about that, but I'm starting to think it was for the better. Where I'm from, all my kids' friends are on drugs. I'm glad to say my kids are okay, at least going to school. One daughter's about to graduate. My other daughter—she's a tough one. Just hope she don't fall into my footsteps. I'm going all in on sobriety, get healthy. Don't want my kids seeing their mom like I am now. It takes jail time for me to slow down and focus on myself. I know what to do; just need some help.

Hardest Thing

How do I know I can trust the judicial system to do the right thing? I turned myself in based on an active warrant, thinking that would be best for my family. I'm now fighting a Child Protection case for the custody of my children. While in jail, my kids were taken from school under the allegation that my baby dad, who had some problems, was living in my home. But that wasn't true because he had been living at a sober house for over a month. Why couldn't the police have checked this out? There are cameras where he lives. When living at home, I was sober and my kids were being taken care of. But my P.O. had a problem with my urine analysis tests. I was on medication, so I stopped taking it. I'm screaming, "HELP," but no one wants to listen. This is the hardest thing I've ever been through in my life. I want to see my kids smile everyday but since I've been gone, they don't smile much during visits.

Illustration: *Only You* by Roberto Lopez-Rios,
Arts from the Inside

Prompt Ten

When I Get Out

> What do I owe the streets? Not this time, I said, when a homey asked me to traffic fetty. Not this time, not next time, not ever. I'm fine being alone and free.

I'm Going

I'm going to be in a place of no pain, tears, or sadness,
Soon as I am free of this madness.
I'm going to be in a lot of trouble if I'm late for the heavy work.
I'm sure that's why my back hurts.
I can't worry about where I came from.
Just got to keep from being a bum.
I won't stop until I complete this race.
I'm running toward a heavenly place.

Nope

Nope, the jury didn't see the facts.
Nope, I'm not sad but mad.
Nope, the system isn't fair—not even close.
Nope, the general public doesn't care until they are sucked into the criminal system vortex.
Nope, I'm not going to end here.
Nope, you can't crush me; it's just a couple of chapters of life.
Nope, when I'm done, I'll bring back justice and reform.

Perfect Day

When these hell gates open,
gray clouds will go away.
The sun will be at the highest point.
My day would not be spent alone.
It will be with my woman and those I love the most.
The night will be filled with candlelight and romance close to the lake.
Flowers and rose petals will bring the ambience while soft melodies play.
My day will be beyond a dream.
Imagination will drip like ice cream—
a day they can't take away from me.

What I Want

I want ten Cadillacs and a diamond mill,
ten suits for clothes and dressed to kill.
I want a ten-room house and some barbecue
and fifty chicks not over twenty-two.
Some catfish fingers and baked mac 'n cheese,
and a woman with a little waist I can squeeze.
I want a lifetime affair and an affair of a lifetime;
I'm ready to shine and leave the old me behind.

Hugs

It will surely be a beautiful day when I get out of jail and can hug my children again. I miss feeling their little bodies wrapped up in my arms, hearing them tell me they love me. Geez, this whole situation is so sad. I could've potentially hurt them—the most beautiful gift from God. I love them more than I ever could've imagined I could love someone.

Running

When I get out, my plan is to get a good job and a place of my own to lay my head. I plan on fixing anything I broke and making amends to anyone I've hurt. When I'm out, I'll be a better person and make better choices. I'm gonna hit the ground running like so many times before.

How Do I Know?

How do I know I'll be okay when I get out?
How do I know I'll recover from this horrible time in my life?
How do I know I'll be done with this lifestyle?
How do I know I won't rebound back to jail?
How do I escape the world of hurt I've built for
myself?
I'm just hoping my parents, children, and boyfriend will
welcome me home.

Messy

My life is messy; I can't wait for it to be cleaned up.
Cops.
Booking.
Jail.
My hair.
My mind.
People.
Men.

Self-Care

Bubble baths, massages, pedicures, and nails
Pampering, love, tenderness, comfort
Facials, waxing, aromas, coloring
Soothing, calm, organized, easy
Simple things known and shared by everyday women and the stars.
Need to put a thousand miles between me and these dreary bars.

Change

I plan on going through with my probation. I'm tired of looking over my shoulder because of active warrants that eventually pop up because of not finishing, or leaving, my programs. I have done this repeating the last few years. It's getting old and time to change.

Not wrong

I am beautiful, I am serene
I am peaceful, I am clean
Satan you're losing your steam
I'll let the almighty intervene
I love you all, I know what I am
I'm human, we do what we can
I am strong and confident
Above all, I'm most resilient
Today, I'll sing your righteous song
I am free and I'm not wrong.

Ten Years

I really can't imagine my future. I am facing a felony charge that could put me in prison for the next ten years. I pray for the best but am prepared for the worst. I have a beautiful supportive family that is behind me 100%. I have six kids that depend on me like crazy and need me more than ever, especially my girls. It's scary not knowing how things will shake out for me and my family ten years from now. Hopefully, we'll be together and I'll be back working, doing positive things with my life.

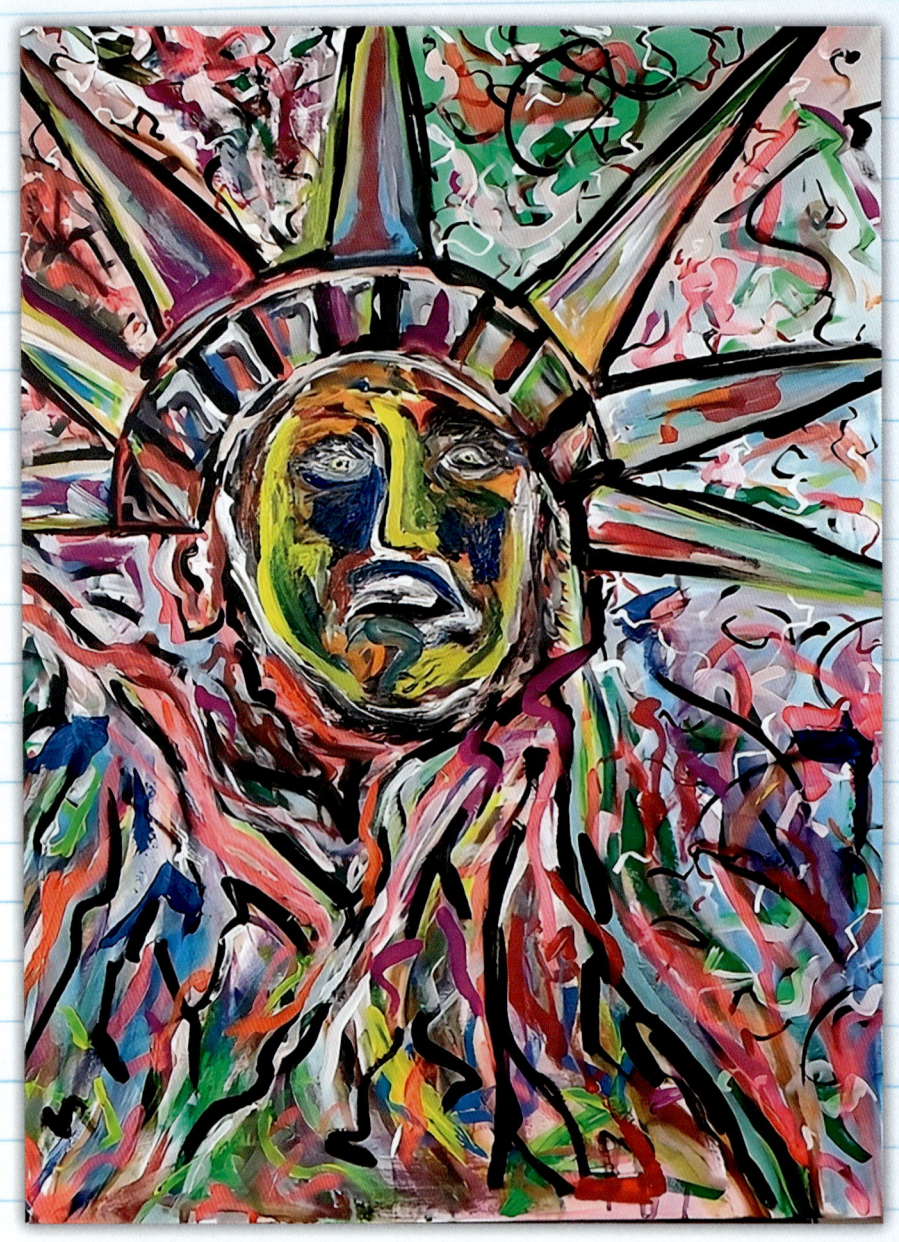

Illustration: *Liberty* by Ricardo Dominguez, Arts from the Inside

Prompt Eleven

Dear Congressman Phillips

> ❝

On April 3, 2023, Congressman Phillips from Minnesota's 3rd congressional district, participated in a FreeWriters session, at the Hennepin County Jail. The following are reflections of the visit, written by the detainees of Quad 11.

Vision

I thank you for taking the time out of your busy schedule to come and pay us a visit at Hennepin County Jail. I am truly blessed to have met someone so influential in our government. I truly believe my stay here in jail was meant to be after your visit. I would love to be able to assist you in any shape or form to further push your vision and/or agenda. I am highly educated, empathetic, and have a very strong work ethic. I wish you well in your endeavors. I hope you remember me, as I will always remember you. God bless you.

Mental Health

Your visit touched me in ways I didn't know it could. Mental health is a big thing these days, and everyone thinks a pill is some sorta answer. I speak for the unspoken. We've had enough and are tired of medical people pissing down our back and telling us it's raining. Let our mental health be a drug-free ride, like the FreeWriters program. It has me thinking straight, and I didn't have to take a pill to get there. Give us some money and open this thing up.

Emotions

We all came out of our seven-by-nine cells thinking it was a regular day of FreeWriters. Ms. G told us to get our asses moving (she's very humorous) and said we have a special guest today. When she expressed it was you and the reason behind it, we all took it very seriously and dug down deep to pull out the respect and manners our mommas taught us. Meeting you was a real cool experience. I have much gratitude for you allowing us to express to you our emotions and the great benefits of the FreeWriters program. Also, seeing you get comfortable in the class and open up to us about your life made me think that you also saw the benefits of FreeWriters. I hope you extend a hand and support the cause one hundred percent.

P.S. I just wish I got to leave with you and had my freedom back.

White House

It was an opportunity to meet you in the first place. I really appreciate you showing up at Hennepin County Jail. I never met any government members since I made it to the United States from Sierra Leone, West Africa. I once visited the White House in 2001, when President Bush was in office, but I didn't make it inside. So, it was a great honor to meet with you, shake hands, and listen to my journal and yours. I just want you to know you gave me hope of visiting you at the White House one day after I finish my book. Perhaps together we can help the homeless and the kids in my country with school supplies.

Power

The power you have is to help people that may not be able to help themselves. The people in jail. Those people. So, thank you.

Brown Men

Hey, thanks for showing up and being part of the FreeWriters class. It's a shock to have someone of much importance come and see how this class of ours works and what it means to us. Being brown men in orange, we look forward to the possible help you could bring the jail programs and FreeWriters. It's appreciated, and thanks again.

Politician

That was my first time meeting a politician. I thought, "This man is going to waste my time and is only doing it for the publicity, like many other politicians." So, I was surprised that you came and were actually happy to be here and were engaged with us. The congressman changed my view on politicians as well as my view on the US. Thank you for taking time out of your day for seeing someone like me.

66

Why?

Mr. Congressman thanks for the visit, can you please answer my questions?

Why is that if you don't have a stash of cash to post bond, you're jailed, and if you do, you're out walkin about?

Why is it that 80% of the detainees in this jail are people of color?

Why are we made to suffer in isolation for extended periods because of staff shortages?

Why is it that you gotta carry a gun on the street to keep yourself and family safe?

Why are poisonous illegal drugs allowed to flow freely and ruin our children's future?

Why are we prohibited from joining the military just because we got in trouble as a teenager?

Why can't voting while in prison be considered part of our civic rehabilitation?

Change

You impress me as someone who works honestly to change things for the better. I want to change things too. Change my thinking from negative to positive. Change my residence from jail to home. Change from self-only to helping people in need. It feels good to help others, but you already know that. I want to make my family and my woman proud of me. I want to be a stand-up man. I want to be done with the bull shit little games. I want to live with no regrets and keep moving forward and get closer to god.

Illustration: *Free Inside, Self Portrait* by Jamal Biggs, Jamal Biggs Fine Art Studio

Prompt Twelve

Mindful Writing

> The yellow stubby pencil primes my desert brain, releasing dammed up tears that fall, blat-blat-blat, onto the lined paper soaking me in long abandoned hope.

"

Why I write. I write because it's therapudict to me. I write because sometimes the man I am on the inside is not the same as the man I allow to be seen on the outside where it might seem I'm tough, really I just don't want to be hurt again so I push people away even the ones I love the most. Writing music or writing in my journal helps to soothe the beast inside.

I think the Freewriters class is and can be ~~this~~ helpful to many people even on the streets it helped me get a start on the book I'm writing and I would like to help build the program in the DOC if possible.

>

I think this is a good class to take peoples mind off what they're going through in here or how they feel! takes your mind else where!

I am glad I came and I know you get people asking for your help all the time. I don't think it's by chance I came, but can you please give me an oppertunity to tell you my story and give me any advice and or resources? Overall, what you are doing is great and opening up our minds.

It helps greatly to make me feel better about this hell hole.

"

I think this is a good program for people who need to stay sober. I will use this program when I'm out and would like to introduce others, who are struggling, to FreeWriters.

The class is really helpful as far as getting your thoughts and burdens of the mind & heart. I request this class specifically because I love to write! Tina is a very inspirational writing coach, and I appreciate her taking the time to let us empty out our thoughts.

"

The writing exercises cracked me open like a dropped egg and allowed me to look at my shattered self. The writings revealed a hardened heart not trusting in love; an ego that fenced off vulnerability; a body absorbed in layers of trauma; circular thoughts to nowhere. I have a long way to go, but Freewriters put me on a journey of salvation, with no return.

I thought this class was absolutely amazing! I was estatic with the option to write!

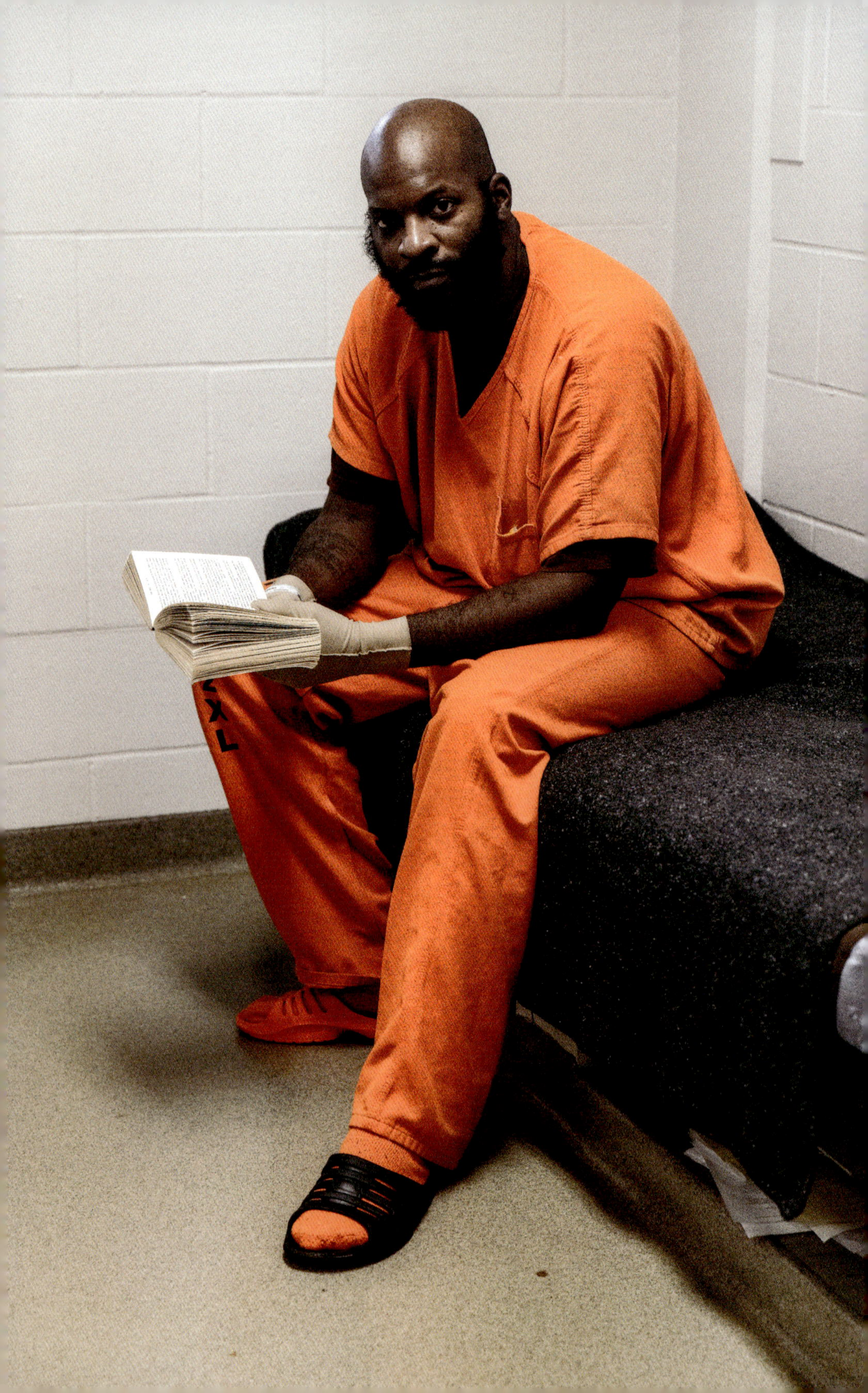

The On-Ramp To Success

An opportunity to recast one's destiny.

Detainees will often confide that the jail experience was a forced, yet welcomed, time-out from substance abuse and an opportunity to assess the consequences of unskillful behavior. In addition, they credit the FreeWriters mindful writing sessions with providing the necessary hope and self-esteem to move positively forward upon release. Of course, that's just the beginning.

It's at the point of release where the rubber hits the road.

During a FreeWriters session, a repeat jail detainee provided insight into the uncertainty of post-jail detention.

Two steps out of jail a roman candle sun lights up my brain.
Sniffing the air, I catch the scent of a BBQ food truck.
I'm stilled by the random sound of chirping birds, a siren and laughter.
This feels like freedom but where do I go from here?

A detainee's post-incarceration success is highly dependent on in-jail re-entry programs and an accessible support network upon release. Unlike prisons, where there are opportunities for mental health and vocational programs, the jail system provides very little in the way of pre- and post-release support.

There is simply no bridge from jail back into the community.

Part of the issue is that those confined in jail stay for unpredictable lengths of time and aren't necessarily there long enough to participate in a full-course program. Programs in jail regularly lose participants as charges against them are dropped, detainees accept plea bargains, or they receive longer sentences that send them to prisons.

This population is not insignificant. Nearly 520,000 people are currently being held in local U.S. jails according to a 2023 report from Prison Policy Initiative. The median bail to secure release for a felony is $10,000. For many pre-trial detainees this amount represents eight months' income, so it's of no surprise bail can't be met.

Further, a survey conducted by the National Alliance to End Homelessness revealed a significant relationship between incarceration and homelessness. More than three-quarters of the homeless surveyed had been incarcerated at some point during their lives. And in the six months before becoming homeless, 43% were in jail or were on probation or parole. The vast majority of those who had been incarcerated received no help signing up for housing, healthcare, or benefits upon release.

Why are so many people detained in jails before trial? They're not wealthy enough to afford money bail.

Median annual pre-incarceration incomes (in 2015 dollars) for people ages 23-39 in local jails who were unable to post a bail bond, compared to incomes of same-age non-incarcerated people, by gender

	Men		Women	
	Detained pretrial	Not incarcerated	Detained pretrial	Not incarcerated
Annual income	$15,598	$39,600	$11,071	$22,704

Median bail amount $10,000

For detailed data notes, see *Detaining the Poor* at www.prisonpolicy.org/reports/incomejails.html

PRISON POLICY INITIATIVE

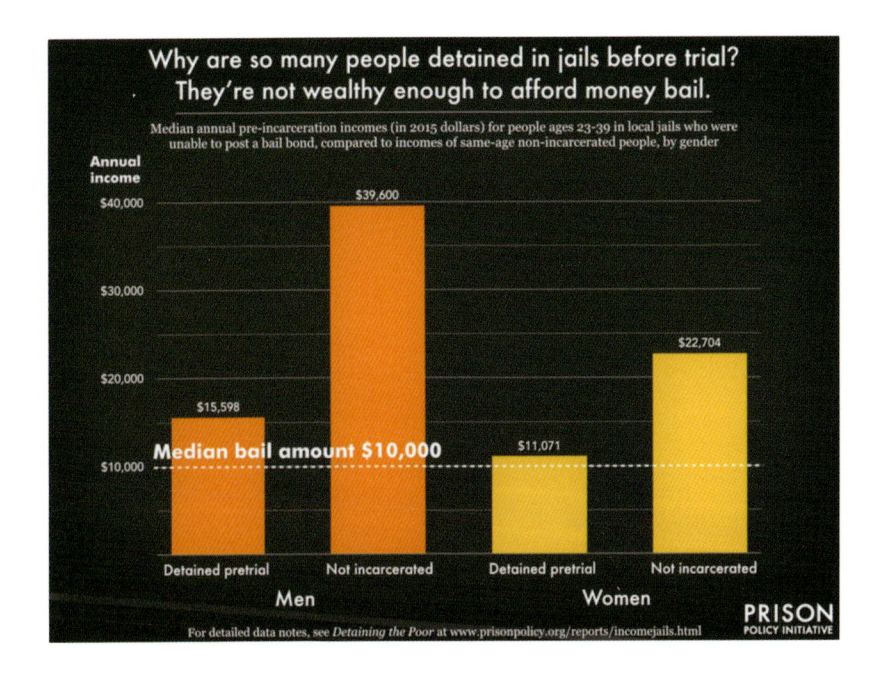

FreeWriters' evolving mission is to facilitate an on-ramp to post-detention programs.

FreeWriters is in a unique position to connect with the hard-to-reach and underserved jail population. Our therapeutic mindful writing practice provides a front-row seat to the issues facing detainees in the post-release world. Through early intervention, it is Free-Writers' intention to facilitate program applications before and after detainees are released. This includes connecting them with housing organizations, food banks, mental health counseling, education, and job resources, ensuring that when they hit the street, they know the route to re-entry success and beyond.

FreeWriters needs your support to make this happen!

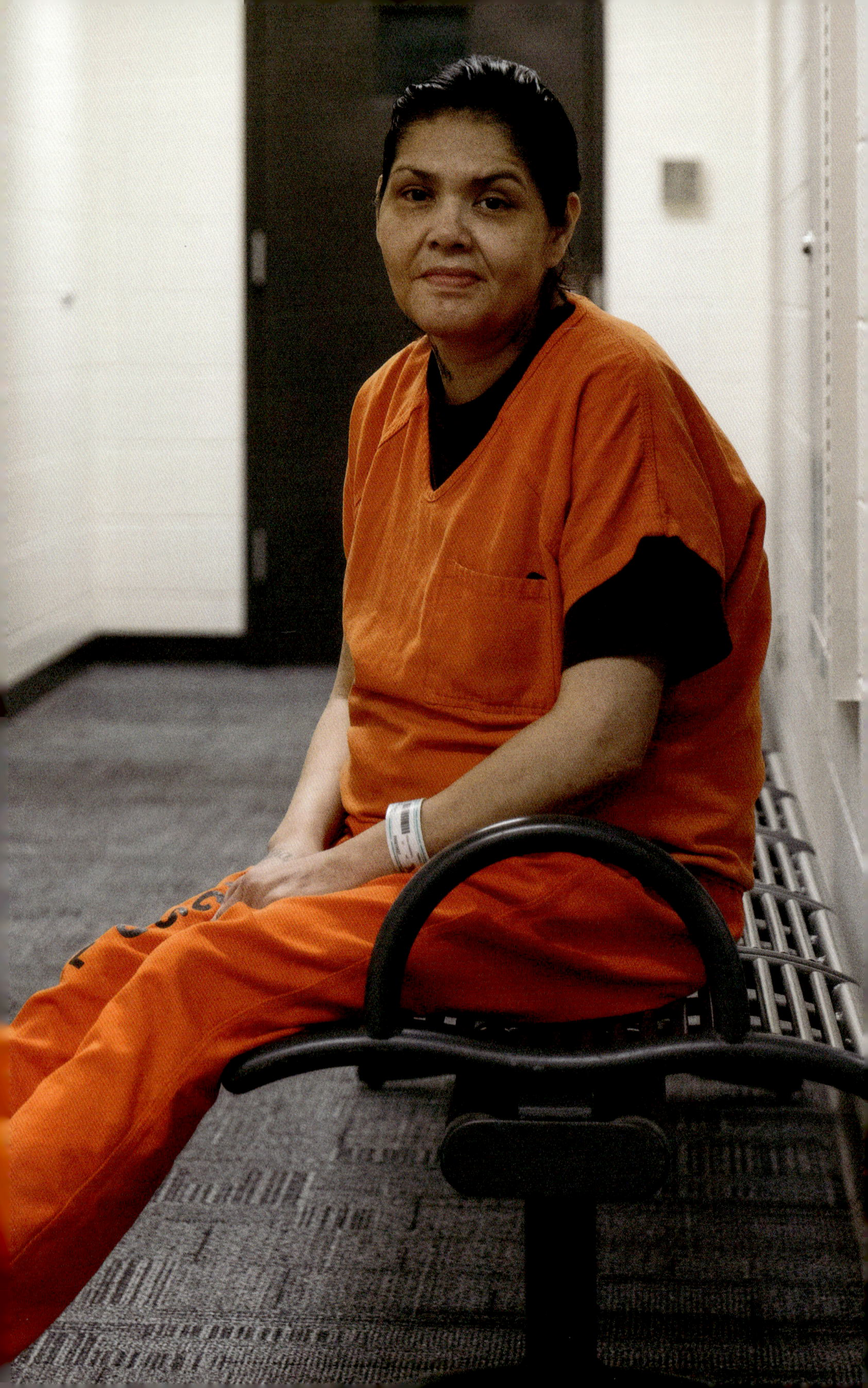

Acknowledgments

Board of Directors

Nate Johnson (ex oficio)
Anicenetta Caldwell (chair)
Melissa Martinez
Armel Green
Melissa Caffes
Damian Johansson
Dr. John Schlueter
Joseph Bunce

FreeWriters Staff

Nate Johnson
Melissa Martinez
Laura Mawe
Joe Bunce
Norma Bourland
Bella Deschene
Nina Resor

FreeWriters Instructors

Nate Johnson
Jenn Kudelka
Dennis Kelly
Norma Bourland
Dr. John Schlueter
Katie Pierson
Doran Schoeppach
Melissa Martinez
Brandon Sutton
Chris Elias
Anthony Walsh
Laura Oakes
Anita Muldoon

Art and Photo Contributors

Art from the Inside, featuring artists **S. Kilman, Ricardo Dominguez and Roberto Lopez-Rios**, is a Minnesota organization that gives incarcerated artists the opportunity to express themselves through art—giving them a visual voice. Arts from the Inside exhibits their art with the hope to inspire dialogue about the complexities of our criminal justice system. https://artfromtheinsidemn.org

Justice Arts Coalition (JAC), featuring artists **Brian Hindson, Zhi Kai H. Vanderford, and Kenneth Reams**, unites teaching artists, arts advocates and artists who are or have been incarcerated, and their allies, harnessing the transformative power of the arts to reimagine justice. https://thejusticeartscoalition.org

Jamal Biggs Fine Art Studio. Jamal firmly believes that because an individual is in prison, it doesn't have to mean he can't still be of value to his family and community, and have dreams and aspirations to become a better human being. His paintings and drawings seek to reflect this duality of a person searching for identity in a society that wants to make him irrelevant and finds him unworthy of self-respect. http://jamalbiggs.com

The Right of Return Fellowship was co-founded by justice-impacted artists **Russell Craig and Jesse Krimes**. It was established by artists, for artists as the first and only national initiative dedicated to supporting and mentoring formerly incarcerated creatives. Right of Return Fellows produce work that advances criminal and racial justice. https://rightofreturnusa.com

Arts By Wash is dedicated to showcasing the original works of the self-taught and wrongfully convicted artist **Fulton Leroy Washington, a.k.a. Mr. Wash**, and supporting criminal justice reform. https://artbywash.com. Mr Wash's mission is funded by **Help Us Help Wash**, a not-for-profit organization seeking to expand awareness and support for the innocent. http://helpushelpwash.org.

Photo Contributors

David Guttenfelder is a photojournalist and *National Geographic* explorer focusing on geopolitical conflict, conservation, and culture. Guttenfelder is an eight-time World Press Photo Award winner and a seven-time finalist for the Pulitzer Prize. http://www.davidguttenfelder.com. Photo credits: pages iii(b), xiv, xxi, xxvi, 90, 94, 102(b).

Damian Johansson is a published writer, teacher and photographer. He currently teaches at the University of St. Thomas, St. Cloud State, and Minneapolis College. His work has been published in *Anamesa* at NYU, *Juxtaprose*, *Rootstalk* (Grinnell College), *The McNeese Review*, and anthologized in *plain china*. He has been featured on NBC Nightly News with Kevin Tibbles. Photo credits: pages iii(a,c,d,), iv, xv, xxx, xxxi, 91, 102(a,d,e).

Community Supporters

Hennepin County Sheriff's Office
Anoka County Sheriff's Office
Wright County Sheriff's Office
Ramsey County Sheriff's Office
Magers & Quinn Booksellers
All Square
Stevens Square Community
    Organization

Funders

Minnesota State Arts Board
Metropolitan Regional Arts
    Council
Westminster Presbyterian Church
Palomar Holdings
Hennepin County
Anoka County
City of Minneapolis
Central Minnesota Jobs and
    Training Services
Unity Church-Unitarian

Donors

Deb Ahmann
Teresa Alto
Richard Anderson
John Apolloni
Rob Armstrong
Christopher Beall
Joanne Bergman
Norma Bourland
Anne Brafford
Kathleen Bruns
Paula Buckner
Kathleen Buhle
Mike Buttry
Jon Christianson
Lorinda Clausen
Tom Cook
Barbara Cronmiller
Dennis and Nickie Dillon
Sandy Donaldson
Judy Ericksen
Hope Esparolini
Diane Foster
Jeffrey Frost
Sieglinde Gassman
Tania Gaxiola
Emily Gleason
Kathy & Hazen Graves
Ella Haidos
Karen Harwitt
Elizabeth Heefner
Kathy and Tim Horner
Peggy Hunter
AngelaJacques
MeganJacques
Greg Johnson
Michelle Johnson
NathanJohnson
Paul Johnson
Sally Johnson
Justin Kelly
Chad and Jessica Kelly
Christine Kirkpatrick
John Kostouros
Kenneth Kraemer

Diana Ky
Mark Lehman
Akeyah Lucas
Nancy and Rom Marczka
Gail Martin
Mary McCain
Emily McChesney
Brenden McGibbon
Marie Monson
Ruth Monson
Jane Moren
Kim Moren
Stephanie Muller
Bridie Musser
Laura Oakes
RachelOelke
Madeline Ortega
Ann Marie Osborne
Meghan and Darryl Pardi
Brigitte Parenteau
Saunya Peterson
Sam Quattrochi
Beau RaRa
Kelly Regan
Cheryl Rogers
Jen Rohde
Mimi Samuel
Elizabeth Simpson
Shelley Snell
Amy Sparks
Janet Sterling
Ann Tanous
Rosemary Taylor
Tracy Tuong
Emily Turner
Quang Van
Katie Walter
Suzanne Weinstein
Brian Weller
Mae Whitney
Pamela Williams
Christina Zauhar Anderson
Gregory Zoidis

Your Support Matters

We need your contributions so we may continue our work. Thank you!

TO DONATE

By making your generous gift, you will receive periodic updates from FreeWriters about how you have made an impact in the lives of those seeking a meaningful path forward from jail.

**To make an online donation,
visit: https://freewriters.org/donate**

To donate by mail, make check payable to:

FreeWriters
P.O. Box 7345
Minneapolis, MN 55407

FOLLOW US ON SOCIAL MEDIA

Facebook: https://www.facebook.com/FreeWritersMinnesota

Instagram: https://www.instagram.com/freewritersmn

TO HOST A FREEWRITERS FUNDRAISING EVENT OR REQUEST A SPEAKER

Contact: info@freewriters.org

TO VOLUNTEER

If you are interested in contributing your time and skill, please contact us at info@freewriters.org

FOR BOOK ORDERS

Online print or ebook, visit Amazon, Barnes & Noble, and Independent Booksellers.

Hard cover singles and bulk orders contact us at info@freewriters.org

FreeWriters is a fully tax-exempt 501(c)3 nonprofit organization. IRS Tax ID# 84-3486930.

"I offer my sincere appreciation and gratitude for the many hands that made this collection of writings possible:

- the hands of the jail personnel who opened their doors to us.
- the hands of volunteers who wrote side by side with the detainees.
- the hands of those in jail who bravely contributed and allowed us to publish their writing.
- the hands of the FreeWriters staff, editorial assistants, board members, community funders and individual donors.

These hands have helped create a magnificent tapestry of diverse stories woven from threads of joy and sorrow, triumphs and challenges, love and loss. Some of these stories will fade away with the passage of time. It is our hope others will be etched in your heart compassionately forever."

Executive Editor and Curator
Dennis Kelly

Dennis is a marketing professional who has been engaged by Fortune 500 companies, not-for-profit organizations and Olympic Committees to provide critical strategic planning and implementation. He is also passionate about writing. His latest award-winning novel reached No. 1 in the Amazon Satire Fiction category. As a mindful writing instructor and coach, he incorporates the practices of meditation, Tai Chi, and of course, humor. He believes that when we laugh at our own foibles, it allows us to reflect on what it means to be human and better cope with the world.

https://denniskellywriter.com

Hennepin

FREEWRITERS.ORG
HENNEPIN COUNTY JAIL - XL
HENNEPIN COUNTY JAIL - XL
HENNEPIN COUNTY JAIL - 4XL
HENNEPIN